MARY
WOMAN AND MOTHER

Francis J. Moloney sdb

WIPF & STOCK · Eugene, Oregon

Wipf and Stock Publishers
199 W 8th Ave, Suite 3
Eugene, OR 97401

Mary
Woman and Mother
By Moloney, Francis J.
Copyright©1988 by Moloney, Francis J.
ISBN 13: 978-1-60608-965-1
Publication date 7/15/2009
Previously published by St. Paul Publications, 1988

For Mary Moloney
(née O'Connor)
Woman and Mother

Preface

The place of Mary within the belief and practice of the Christian Churches has been a matter of debate since the days of the Reformation.[1] In the years since the Second Vatican Council, which closed in 1965, many have noticed an apparent shift of direction in Roman Catholic interest in Mary, paralleled by a renewed attention to her from the Protestant traditions. This is but one of the many fruits of the Council. All the Christian Churches are turning more readily to a reading of the Sacred Scriptures together, as we share what unites us. The person of Mary as she comes to us from the pages of the New Testament is proving to be, despite centuries of division, an instrument for such unity.

In 1974 Paul VI indicated the contemporary orientation of Catholics towards an increased use of the Bible as its 'basic prayer-book', concluding that:

> Devotion to the Blessed Virgin cannot be exempt from this general orientation of Christian piety; indeed it should draw inspiration in a special way from this orientation in order to gain new vigour and sure help (*Marialis Cultus* 30).

Continuing the initiative of Paul VI, the encyclical letter *Redemptoris Mater* of John Paul II is an attempt 'to emphasise the *special presence* of the Mother of God in the mystery of Christ and his Church' (*Redemptoris Mater* 48. Stress in original). Such an emphasis is important for several reasons: the above-mentioned ecumenical dimensions of the question, the seeming decrease in 'popular Marian piety', especially in Europe, and the growing awareness of the importance of woman in the Christian Churches would be some of these.

Whatever the reasons, the Christian Churches have been increasingly urged to reflect upon the role and place of Mary within the context of the Christian mystery and as an important subject for devotion and for the development of a Christian spirituality. Any reflecting Christian cannot ignore this summons. We are at a stage

---

[1] For a documented study, see G. Söll, *Storia dei Dogmi Mariani* (Accademia Mariana Salesiana XV; Rome: LAS, 1981) pp. 409-416.

in all the Churches where questions are being raised and paths of investigation and reflection are being indicated. The work which follows is an attempt to respond to the challenge through a study of the New Testament portrait of Mary, the woman and the mother of Jesus.

After a more general discussion of the place, the value and the limitations of an explicitly New Testament study of Mary, I have followed what I regard to be the historical development of the documents of the New Testament. I have analysed passages from St Paul's Letter to the Galatians, the Gospels of Mark, Matthew and Luke, the Acts of the Apostles and the Gospel of John which make explicit reference to Mary, the mother of Jesus. It appears to me that one can trace a developing appreciation and theology of Mary, as a mother and a woman, through these pages. I have then drawn some conclusions and asked some questions which have necessarily arisen from the Mariology which comes to us from the inspired and foundational documents of the early Church.

I am most grateful to the many people who have led me through this study: to my students of Mariology at Catholic Theological College, Clayton and to the Salesian Biblical Association, which demanded that I present a paper on these questions for their Second International Congress in Rome. I am also grateful to Sister Emanuel Saccoman, FSP, who read the first draft of the manuscript, and Sister Margaret Jenkins, CSB, who read the penultimate draft. Both of these women added their intuition and encouragement to my scholarship.

Fr. Michael Goonan of the Society of St Paul made some important suggestions which enabled me to give the final draft its present shape. He also saw the work through the various stages of its production. To him I am particularly grateful.

It is lovingly dedicated to my own mother, another Mary, from whom I have learnt – and thankfully continue to learn – so much about the ways of God. Even in these late years of her journey, she goes on accepting all the surprises, both painful and joyful, which the Lord sends into her life. In this she both teaches and serves us all.

Salesian Theological College
Oakleigh, Victoria 3166   *Francis J. Moloney, SDB*
14th February 1988.

Contents

Chapter 1

The Place of a New Testament Reflection on Mary

Following the correct intuition of Paul VI's *Marialis Cultus*, the Bible must be the starting point for a renewed Christian reflection upon Mary. The Bible is indeed our major source of 'new vigour and sure help' (*Marialis Cultus* 30). Yet it is important – as we begin our New Testament reflections on Mary – to realise the limitations of a purely biblical study. It cannot hope to tell the whole story. The presentation of the person and role of Mary in the New Testament is only the *beginnings* of Christian reflection upon the mystery of the Mother of Jesus.

We should not be surprised to find that the New Testament does not contain all the Marian teaching and practice which has developed over the centuries.[1] We must allow the New Testament to be what it is: the inspired and inspiring reflection and teaching of the earliest Church. Once we allow that, then we will neither search for, nor discover through forced or subtle interpretations of the biblical text, the Church's later Marian doctrines. The great Marian dogmas which have developed over the centuries must not be presupposed in the documents which have come down to us from the earliest decades of the existence of Christian communities.[2]

---

[1] In fact, two important Catholic Marian teachings were defined as such quite recently. The Immaculate Conception of Mary was solemnly defined by Pope Pius IX in 1854, and the Assumption of Mary by Pope Pius XII in 1950. Of course, while these later dogmas are not explicitly found in the Scriptures, Catholic tradition claims that they flow from and never contradict the biblical data. This is an area of important and sometimes difficult ecumenical debate. See, for some reflections, J. Ratzinger, *Daughter Zion. Meditations on the Church's Marian Belief* (San Francisco: Ignatius Press, 1983) pp. 31-37; A. J. Tambasco, *What are they saying about Mary?* (New York: Paulist Press, 1984) pp. 13-37.

[2] The tendency to 'find' later doctrines in the Marian passages from the New Testament has been caricatured by R. Haughton, *The Re-Creation of Eve* (Springfield: Templegate Publishers, 1985) p. 110: 'A nodding acquaintance with Marian literature shows the writers (almost always male) beginning with the theologically developed picture of the Sinless One, the Second Eve, and then fitting the Gospel incidents into it, even at the cost of amazingly complicated explanations of the text'. This is a dangerous practice, given the fact that the great doctrines of the Church took several centuries to develop in a Greco-Roman world which was very different from the world of the New Testament.

Although it is important that the reader be warned against seeking too much in the New Testament, a further more positive note needs to be sounded. In the documents of the New Testament we have only the *written* record of the faith and practice of the early Church. It does not tell us the whole story of the faith and its articulation in those earliest years. The preaching of Paul and the narratives about the life and teaching of Jesus which we have within the pages of the New Testament are only *part* of the preaching and the story-telling that went on in those critical, formative years.

There was much more going on, and it was alive in the oral traditions of the Church through the early centuries. These traditions gathered strength, purified through the preaching of the word and the experience of Christian life.[3] They eventually came to receive a great variety of written expressions in the Greek, Syrian and Latin Fathers of the Church.[4]

At least early in the second century, but most probably even before that, in New Testament times themselves,[5] profound and creative

On this period, see F. Young, *From Nicea to Chalcedon. A Guide to the Literature and its Background* (London: SCM Press, 1983). Dealing specifically with the Marian dogmas, see G. Söll, *Storia dei Dogmi Mariani* pp. 79-170.

[3] The Fathers of the Church and the apocryphal material show knowledge of important ancient oral material. Eusebius (*The History of the Church* 39.1) quotes Papias (circa 60-130AD) as writing: 'For I did not imagine that things out of books would help me as much as the utterance of a living and abiding voice' (Translation from G. A. Williamson's Eusebius, *The History of the Church from Christ to Constantine* [Minneapolis: Augsburg, 1975] p. 150). Of course, care must be taken in the use of the apocryphal material. See, for some suggestions on the positive use of this non-canonical material, C. Drury, 'Who's In, Who's Out', in M. Hooker – C. Hickling (eds.), *What about the New Testament? Essays in Honour of Christopher Evans* (London: SCM Press, 1975) pp. 223-233.

[4] For studies of the Marian thought of the Fathers, see the surveys of W. Burghardt, 'Mary in Western Patristic Thought', *Mariology* 1 (1955) 109-155; Idem, 'Mary in Eastern Patristic Thought', *Mariology* 2 (1957) 88-153. See also R. Laurentin's 'Bulletin marial' which has appeared twice yearly in *Revue des Sciences Philosophiques et Théologiques* since 1962, and E. Carroll's 'Survey of Recent Mariology' which appears annually in *Marian Studies*.

[5] The New Testament documents often seem to be doing battle with some form of Christian thought which was at odds with that of the community which produced the document in question. This is generally taken for granted in Pauline studies, although it can often be difficult to establish exactly which position Paul is attacking. We have only one side of the argument in Paul's letters. On this, see C. Hickling, 'On Putting Paul in his Place', in *What about the New Testament?*, pp. 76-88. Current Marcan studies devote a lot of attention to the 'heresy' which occasioned that Gospel. For a survey, see J. D. Kingsbury, *The Christology of Mark's Gospel* (Philadelphia: Fortress Press, 1983) pp. 1-45. The Fourth Gospel and the Johannine Epistles show that debate was in full swing. See, for example, the suggestions of R. E. Brown, *The Community of the Beloved Disciple. The Lives, Loves and Hates of an Individual Church in New Testament Times* (London: Geoffrey Chapman, 1979).

thinkers began to speculate upon the texts of the Bible, and the other traditions which had gone before them, to produce systems of thought that seemed to be in conflict with the accepted beliefs of the Christian people at large. Intimately linked with the person of Jesus, their understanding of Mary, his mother, was a central part of these conflicts. These internal debates eventually led to the great Councils of the Church, beginning at Nicea in 325.[6] It was within the context of these great Councils that traditional Marian doctrines were eventually formed.

The debates and the discussions did not cease at Nicea or Chalcedon. Through all the ages the Church has been called to go on teaching her timeless truths through the profound and instructive use of the whole of its tradition, in order to make it relevant to the life of the Church and the individual believer of today. All Christian Churches reach back to the great patrimony of Scripture and Tradition to address the problems and possibilities of the contemporary world with a message which is both age old and ever new.[7] In the Catholic Church, the definition of the Immaculate Conception and the Assumption of Mary, however problematic such doctrines may be in contemporary ecumenical discussions,[8] is an indication of this ongoing development of the teachings of the Church.

Similarly, works of Christian Marian spirituality – in some ways continuing the methods of the great Fathers of the Church – summon an awareness, turning to Scripture and Tradition to produce a white hot message so well described by the prophet Jeremiah: 'There is in my heart as it were a burning fire shut up in my bones, and I am weary with holding it in, and I cannot' (Jer 20:9). Such a response to the word of God in forming and nurturing Marian piety is vital for the life of the Church.[9]

---

[6] For a brief survey of the Church's developing appreciation of Mary's person and place in God's history of salvation and our response to it, see M. B. Pennington, *Mary Today. The Challenging Woman* (New York: Doubleday, 1987) pp. 1-46.

[7] Thus, papal encyclicals have their own 'literary form'. *Redemptoris Mater* is an outstanding example of this. Although Pope John Paul II uses the Vatican Council and the Scriptures as his point of departure (nos 1-6), he does not offer a study of the Council and the New Testament. They are primarily his 'inspiration'.

[8] See, for a survey, A. J. Tambasco, *What are they Saying about Mary?*, pp. 54-64.

[9] See, on this, J. M. Lozano, *Life as Parable. Reinterpreting the Religious Life* (New York: Paulist Press, 1986) pp. 38-48. Again, for a survey of developments in contemporary Marian piety, see A. J. Tambasco, *What are they saying about Mary?*, pp. 65-72.

3

The work on Mary which follows will be limited to a reflection on the texts of the New Testament in which Mary, the woman and the mother of Jesus, plays a role.[10] At no stage will I presuppose the later Catholic Marian dogmas, as I will always attempt to respect the literary and historical contexts of the documents and passages which I am analysing, and which all Christian traditions share. However, while I will not use later developments to interpret the texts, I trust that my Catholic reader will find that I never threaten such later understandings.

The Second Vatican Council asked the Church's teachers and scholars: 'to be careful to refrain as much from all false exaggeration as from too summary an attitude in considering the special dignity of the Mother of God', while it asked the faithful to 'remember moreover that true devotion consists neither in sterile or transitory affection, nor in a certain vain credulity, but proceeds from true faith' (*Lumen Gentium* 67).

The following biblical reflection on Mary, woman and mother, attempts to respond to both of these requests. I hope to uncover, through a faith-directed but critical reading of the New Testament, the woman and the mother who stands at the beginnings of the Christian story. My efforts will, I trust, help readers to deepen not only their appreciation of the full richness of the Marian traditions which form part of the Christian faith, but even more, their lives in the Spirit. After all: 'The words that I have spoken to you are spirit and life' (John 6:63).

---

[10] I will survey the Marian material found in Paul's Letter to the Galatians, Mark, Matthew, Luke and John, as I believe that they appeared in their final form in that chronological order. I am aware that the dating of the documents is still disputed. See especially, J. A. T. Robinson, *Redating the New Testament* (London: SCM Press, 1976).

Chapter 2

The Beginnings
(Paul and Mark):
Woman and Mother

The earliest reference to the Mother of Jesus is found in the Letter to the Galatians: 'But when the time had fully come, God sent forth his Son, born of a woman, born under the law' (Gal 4:4).[1]

Little can be said for a mariological interpretation of this passage, but it is important to notice that a basic affirmation is made: at the beginning of Jesus' life there was a woman, his mother. Paul's interest is to indicate Jesus' authentic Jewishness, something which is communicated through a Jewish mother,[2] but the point is made: there was a woman crucial to the life of Jesus – his mother. It has been suggested that this formula came to Paul from an earlier tradition which, among other things, may have said more about the woman of whom Jesus was born.[3] This reminds us that we no longer have all that the early Church said and thought on these – and many other – matters. Our biblical reflection, however, must be limited to what Paul communicated through Gal 4:4: Jesus was born of a woman, a mother. Although the Christology of the passage is certainly profound,[4] its message about Mary is limited to the facts of her being a woman and a mother.

---

[1] There are difficulties in locating the exact time and place of the writing of Galatians. However, it was certainly written between 50-55. On this see, W. G. Kümmel, *Introduction to the New Testament* (London: SCM Press, 1975) pp. 298-304.

[2] See, on this, H.-D. Betz, *Galatians* (Hermeneia; Philadelphia: Fortress, 1979) pp. 207-208; H. Schlier, *Lettera ai Galati* (Biblioteca di Studi Biblici 3; Brescia: Paideia, 1965) pp. 201-203; F. F. Bruce, *The Epistle to the Galatians. A Commentary on the Greek Text* (The New International Greek Testament Commentary; Exeter: Paternoster Press, 1982) pp. 194-196; J. Ratzinger, *Daughter Zion*, pp. 38-40. For a summary, see R. E. Brown – K. P. Donfried – J. A. Fitzmyer – J. Reumann (eds.), *Mary in the New Testament* (London: Geoffrey Chapman, 1978) pp. 41-45.

[3] See R. H. Fuller, 'The Conception/Birth of Jesus as a Christological Moment', *Journal for the Study of the New Testament* 1 (1978) 37-52 (esp. pp. 40-41). See also E. Schweizer, art. 'huios', *TDNT* VIII (1972) 374-376. For a summary, see F. F. Bruce, *The Epistle to the Galatians*, p. 195.

[4] See the commentaries mentioned in note 3.

5

The same point is made in the earliest of the Gospels: the Gospel of Mark, where Mary, the mother of Jesus, is explicitly mentioned on two occasions.[5]

The first mention of Mary comes in an overall context marked by Jesus' teaching on the new family of God (3:7 — 6:6a).[6] After the institution of the 'Twelve' (3:13-14) Jesus meets opposition from his own family (3:19b-21) and from the religious leaders of Israel (3:22-30). His own family return in vv. 31-35, again presented in a negative light:[7]

> And his mother and his brothers came; and standing outside they sent to him and called him. And a crowd was sitting about him; and they said to him, 'Your mother and your brothers are outside, asking for you.' And he replied, 'Who are my mother and my brothers?' And looking around on those who sat about him, he said, 'Here are my mother and my brothers! Whoever does the will of God is my brother, and sister and mother' (3:31-35).

Jesus, informed that his mother and brothers are 'outside', looks at those gathered around him, 'inside', listening to his word, and gives a new criteria for belonging to the family of Jesus. The issue is no longer a question of blood or nation, but: 'Whoever does the will of God is my brother and sister, and mother' (3:35).

We must take care not to derive from this passage the idea that Jesus did not care for his mother. That would be to misunderstand the theological issue at stake: to belong to Jesus depends on faith, not on blood. His affection for his mother is not the issue; discipleship is.[8]

There is a further mention of the mother of Jesus, this time giving us her name 'Mary', at the close of this same section of the Gospel

---

5   The Gospel of Mark probably appeared around the year 70. There are good arguments defending a time either just before or just after the fall of Jerusalem. For a survey, see W. G. Kümmel, *Introduction to the New Testament*, pp. 97-98.

6   On this structure, see F. J. Moloney, *The Living Voice of the Gospel. The Gospels Today* (Melbourne: Collins Dove, 1987) pp. 30-31.

7   The technique of 'framing' is typically Marcan. Jesus' own family is presented in a negative light in vv. 13-14, and again in vv. 31-35, framing vv. 22-30. On this technique, see D. Rhoads — D. Michie, *Mark as Story. An Introduction to the Narrative of a Gospel* (Philadelphia: Fortress Press, 1982) p. 51.

8   Luke, who makes Mary the first of all disciples, as we shall see later, radically rewrites this passage from Mark to include Mary among those who 'hear the word of God and do it' (Lk 8:19-21). See, on this, R. E. Brown et alii (eds.), *Mary in the New Testament*, pp. 167-170.

of Mark (6:1-6a). In rejecting Jesus, his own townspeople are able to ask the right questions: 'Where did this man get all this? What is the wisdom given to him? What mighty works are wrought by his hands!' (6:2), but they give the wrong answer. They fail to understand the source of Jesus' authority and power because they believe that they know his *origins*: 'Is not this the carpenter, the son of Mary and the brother of James and Joses and Judas and Simon and are not his sisters here with us?' (6:3). They are unable to recognise the inbreak of the kingdom *of God*, as they recognise him only as the son *of Mary*.[9]

The issue is not Marian, but Christological. We must allow the Marcan message to speak for itself. Here, as throughout the whole of this section of the Gospel (3:7 – 6:6a), the Evangelist Mark is concerned with establishing a theology of a new family of God, able to look beyond the limits of human history and our control of it into God's challenging presence in the person of his Son, Jesus of Nazareth. It is in this theological context that 'Mary' is used to speak of his human mother ... but, for Mark, to know the identity of his mother (or his brothers and sisters[10]) is not enough

---

[9] Some scholars find it striking that only Jesus' mother is mentioned, especially in the light of Mt 13:55, where he is called 'the carpenter's son' and Lk 4:22, where he is called 'Joseph's son'. For example, M. Miguens, *The Virgin Birth. An Evaluation of the Scriptural Evidence* (Westminster: Christian Classics, 1975) p. 21 affirms that Mark knew that Jesus was the exclusive 'Son of God', and thus had to eliminate any reference to Joseph. This is 'the only reason one can think of' for the exclusive reference to Mary in 6:3. There could be other reasons. E. Stauffer, *Jesus and His Story* (London: SCM Press, 1960) pp. 23-25 has suggested that 6:3 was a charge of illegitimacy (see the survey of the later Talmudic material which lays this charge against Jesus in J. Z. Lauterbach, 'Jesus in the Talmud', in T. Weiss-Rossmarin (ed.), *Jewish Expressions on Jesus. An Anthology* [New York: Ktav, 1977] pp. 56-69). Most would suggest that Mark reports only Jesus' mother because Joseph was already deceased. On this, see (from among many) R. Pesch, *Das Markusevangelium* (Herders theologischer Kommentar zum Neuen Testament II/1; Freiburg: Herder, 1977) pp. 318-319.

[10] Catholics are often disturbed by this reference to the 'brothers and sisters' of Jesus as it seems to question the perpetual virginity of Mary. Both the Aramaic and Greek words for brother and sister could mean blood brothers and sisters, and thus those further children of Mary, or the 'extended family' of cousins, aunts and uncles. The New Testament text itself is open to *either* interpretation. The Church's traditional teaching on the perpetual virginity of Mary must guide both the faithful and the exegete in their interpretation of these passages. For an excellent summary of this discussion from the times of the Fathers, see J. B. Lightfoot, *Saint Paul's Epistle to the Galatians* (London: Macmillan, 1884) pp. 252-291. See also the study of the Catholic scholar, J. Blinzler, *Die Brüder und Schwestern Jesu* (Stuttgarter Bibelstudien 21; Stuttgart: Katholisches Bibelwerk, 1967).

fully to understand who Jesus is: the Son of God (see 1:1, 11; 9:7; 15:39).

Yet, even though the passages in Paul and Mark do not indicate any profound reflection on the role of Mary, we are able to rise from our reading of these earliest texts with some all important *facts* established: Jesus was born of a woman: he had a mother, whose name was Mary.

This may appear to be meagre pickings, but I hope to show that the developing New Testament understanding of Mary's place in God's plan relies heavily on these basic issues: Mary, the woman, the mother of Jesus.[11] While there appears to be little reflection on the *theological* significance of Mary in the earliest writings of Paul and Mark, these authors have provided us with some all-important facts. In the later, and more theologically developed, New Testament reflections on Mary she will be presented consistently as a woman and a mother.

---

[11] I am well aware that there are scholars, both Catholic and Protestant, who would like to read quite advanced mariological thinking into these texts, especially as regards Mary's virginity. See, for example, H. E. W. Turner, 'Expository Problems: The Virgin Birth', *The Expository Times* 68 (1956-57) 12; J. McHugh, *The Mother of Jesus in the New Testament* (London: Darton, Longman & Todd, 1975) pp. 175-176 (on Paul), pp. 235-247 (on Mark); M. Miguens, The Virgin Birth, pp. 46-53 (on Paul), pp. 6-27 (on Mark); C. E. B. Cranfield, *The Epistle to the Romans* (International Critical Commentary; Edinburgh: T. & T. Clark, 1975) p. 59; A. Vanhoye, 'La mère du fils de Dieu selon Ga 4:4', *Marianum* 40 (1978) 237-247; A. Serra, Art. 'Vergine', in S. De Fiores − S. Meo (eds.), *Nuovo Dizionario di Mariologia* (Rome: Edizioni Paoline, 1985) pp. 1425-1429. Serra's article contains an excellent bibliography (pp. 1473-1476). While I do not wish to deny the possibility of early traditions concerning the virgin birth, the arguments advanced to rediscover these traditions, and to make them part of the Pauline or Marcan argument, strain both the grammar and the context in every case. A recent study of the pre-Marcan traditions behind 3:31-35 and 6:3 argues that the opposite was the case: pre-Marcan traditions thought of Jesus' brothers and sisters as genuine blood brothers and sisters. See, L. Oberlinner, *Historische Überlieferungen und christologische Aussage. Zur Frage der 'Brüder Jesu' in der Synopse* (Forschung zur Bibel 19; Stuttgart: Katholisches Bibelwerk, 1975). We must be careful not to force the issue by trying to get too much 'grist for our mill'.

Chapter 3

The Gospel of Matthew: A Woman of Faith

Matthew 12:46-50 simply repeats Mark's message on the new family of Jesus (Mk 3:31-35), and Matthew seems to play down the role of Mary as Jesus' mother in 13:55 by introducing 'the carpenter' as Jesus' father. The Matthean infancy narrative (Mt 1-2) never presents Mary as the main protagonist. The whole of the story is told through the experience of Joseph.[1] These indications of the text itself have led scholars to claim that the Gospel of Matthew shows very little interest in the figure of Jesus' mother, and has nothing to teach us about the early Church's reflection on the person and role of Mary.[2] A careful reading of Mt 1:1-17 shows that this is not the case.[3]

Genealogies are used in the biblical literature to convey more than just the names they list. They are always used to make a point.[4] Matthew announces his genealogy in 1:1 as the 'book of the genealogy' (Greek: *biblos geneseôs*) of Jesus Christ, the Son of David, the Son of Abraham, and he closes it in v. 17 by telling his readers that all the generations (Greek: *hai geneai*) from Abraham to Jesus were consistently fourteen: from Abraham to David, from David to

---

[1] Contemporary scholarship places the writing of the Gospel of Matthew in a largely Jewish-Christian community some time in the 80's of the first century. See the survey of W. G. Kümmel, *Introduction to the New Testament*, pp. 119-120.

[2] See, for example, R. Mahoney, 'Die Mutter Jesu im Neuen Testament', in G. Dautzenberger – H. Merklein – K. Müller (eds.), *Die Frau im Urchristentum* (Quaestiones Disputatae 95; Herder: Freiburg, 1983) pp. 97-103. It is indicative that a book which takes a maximalist approach to the Marian material in the New Testament, J. McHugh, *The Mother of Jesus in the New Testament*, devotes no space to the uniquely Matthean contribution. M. Miguens, *The Virgin Birth*, p. 140 writes of Mt 1-2: 'The theological ideas involved are not those of a developed Christian thought – indeed they are perfectly Jewish and do not go beyond the theology of the Old Testament'. Similarly, R. Haughton, *The Re-Creation of Eve*, p. 111 writes of the Matthean material: 'Mary is simply part of the expected background'. What follows will disagree with these assessments.

[3] For a fuller discussion, see F. J. Moloney, *Woman: First Among the Faithful. A New Testament Study* (Melbourne: Collins Dove, 1984) pp. 33-39.

[4] See R. R. Wilson, 'Between "Azel" and "Azel". Interpreting the Biblical Genealogies', *Biblical Archeologist* 42 (1979) 11-22.

the Exile, from the Exile to the Christ. Whatever one might make of Matthew's mathematics, or the accuracy of his list of names, his theology is clear. He has used an obvious literary scheme of a threefold repetition of fourteen generations to announce that the coming of Jesus, the Christ, was the end result of a long history which has unfolded according to the careful design of God.[5] God has been the director of sacred history, from Abraham to Jesus.

Once we see this carefully constructed list as an indication of Matthew's conviction that God has been the master of a sacred history, another problem emerges: why do we find the names of women in the list, clumsily breaking into the regular pattern of: 'A was the father of B, B was the father of C, C was the father of D'? It looks as if Matthew has disturbed the normal pattern of a genealogy because he wishes to make a point through the introduction of the women. It has long been seen that the solution to this problem will lie in the discovery of some common element(s) which bind all the women together.[6]

St Jerome suggested that all the women were sinners,[7] Martin Luther made popular the theory that they were all foreigners,[8] while more recent scholars have argued that it is a ploy used by Matthew in his debate with the Jewish argument that Jesus had no claims on the Davidic dynasty.[9] While each of these suggestions gives some guidance, they fail to satisfy totally, especially when all *five* women in the genealogy, including Mary, of whom Jesus was born (v. 16), must be accounted for. They are not all sinners, they are not all

---

[5] The use of threefold pattern indicates perfection, but the use of fourteen names is harder to explain. It may be that it has its origins in the use of exactly fourteen names from Abraham to David in I Chron 1-2, or there may be a play on the Hebrew for 'David', which has a numerical value of 14. On these issues, see R. E. Brown, *The Birth of the Messiah. A Commentary on the Infancy Narratives in Matthew and Luke* (New York: Doubleday, 1977) pp. 74-81.

[6] Some refuse to accept any common denominator. See, for example, M. B. Pennington, *Mary Today*, pp. 4-5: 'Perhaps there is no common demoninator here, save the unlikely choices of divine grace' (p. 5).

[7] *In Matthaeum* 9; PL 26:21.

[8] See, on this H. Stegemann, ' "Die des Uria": zur Bedeutung der Frauennamen in der Genealogie von Matthäus 1:1-17, in *Tradition und Glaube* (Festgabe K. G. Kuhn; Göttingen: Vandenhoeck und Ruprecht, 1972) pp. 246-276.

[9] See M. D. Johnson, *The Purpose of the Biblical Genealogies with Special Reference to the Setting of the Genealogies of Jesus* (SNTS Monograph Series 8; Cambridge, University Press, 1969) pp. 152-179.

foreigners, and the debate over the legitimacy of Jesus' Davidic lineage seems to be a later question.[10]

There are three features which can be attributed to all five women:

1. Each of the women mentioned plays a fundamental role at major turning points in the history of God's people. Tamar continues God's line after the death of Er and Onan (see Gen 46:12). Rahab is the heroine at Jericho, where Israel enters the promised land (see Josh 2:1-21; 6:17-25). Ruth is the mother of Obed, the grandfather of David (see Ruth 4:18-22). Bathsheba conceives Solomon by David, and with the guidance of the prophet Nathan establishes her son as the continuation of the Davidic line (see I Kings 1:11 – 2:9). Mary was the woman 'of whom Jesus was born, who is called Christ' (Mt 1:16).

2. In every case there is something irregular in the sexual situation. It was a scandal to those who were outside the mystery of God's plan working through them. That this was the case with Mary is clearly indicated by vv. 18b-19: 'When his mother Mary had been betrothed to Joseph, before they came together she was found to be with child of the Holy Spirit; and her husband Joseph, being a just man, and unwilling to put her to shame, resolved to divorce her quietly'.

3. Despite the irregularities, all of these women, including Mary, showed initiative and courage when they were called by God to preserve the God-willed line of his Messiah. They are all seen by Matthew as integral to God's plan, shown through the strangeness of his ways through the unfolding of history.

Although Matthew devotes little attention to the person of Mary, he provides us with our first important glimpse of the earliest Church's reflection on Mary, the mother of Jesus. Mary is presented as the final and perfect instrument in God's providential history. She brings to fruition a long history of courageous women and mothers, as she gives birth to the Messianic son of David, son of Abraham (see 1:1). Matthew indicates that Israel's sacred history has been marked, from its very beginnings, by women open to God's action in their lives, cost them what it may. The presence of the feminine through the religious history of Israel, incarnated in the

---

[10] On this, see R. E. Brown et alii (eds.), *Mary in the New Testament*, p. 80 and R. E. Brown, *Messiah*, pp. 534-542.

women mentioned explicitly by Matthew, and culminated in Mary of Nazareth, shows that, despite all the judgments of society, religion and culture, they were the ones who were open to the initiative of God working in them. Thus, one of them became the mother of the Messiah.[11]

Joseph Ratzinger has suggested that the whole of the Old Testament is marked by the figure of the woman, and that her presence is indispensable for the structure of biblical faith. Although I have looked back from Mt 1:16 to the women of the Old Testament, and Ratzinger looks from the Old Testament forward towards Mary of Nazareth, his conclusions match mine:

> The figure of the woman, until then seen only typologically in Israel although provisionally personified by the great women of Israel, also emerges with a name: Mary. She emerges as the personal epitome of the feminine principle in such a way that the principle is true only in the person, but the person as an individual always points beyond herself to the all-embracing reality, which she bears and represents.[12]

It is precisely this radical openness to the 'all-embracing reality' of the action of God which will become the *leit-motif* of the Lucan presentation of Mary. Once again we can sense that we are touching something from the unwritten thought and practice of the early Church. There may be differences and even contradictions in the two infancy narratives preserved by Matthew and Luke,[13] and we generally turn uniquely to Luke for our portrait of Mary. To ignore the contribution of Matthew is to miss the point that his long story of 'women', perfected in the final compromise of the woman Mary, has shown us an important advance on the themes which we discovered in Paul and Mark.

The earliest Church immediately saw Mary as a woman and a mother. These themes are repeated in Matthew, but now we see Mary understood and presented as the perfection of all the women who have played a decisive role in the gradual unfolding of God's

---

[11] This is a profoundly Christian theological insight, despite the claims of M. Miguens, *The Virgin Birth*, pp. 134-141 and R. Haughton, *The Re-Creation of Eve*, p. 111. See above, note 2.

[12] J. Ratzinger, *Daughter Zion*, pp. 27-28. His sensitive reflection on the feminine in the Old Testament is found on pp. 9-29.

[13] For an assessment, see F. J. Moloney, 'The Infancy Narratives. Another View of Raymond Brown's *The Birth of the Messiah*', *The Clergy Review* 65 (1979) 161-166.

salvation history to become the mother of Jesus Christ. Tamar, Rahab, Ruth and Bathsheba are not only *women* of great significance in critical moments in God's unfolding plan for his people. There is more to their role: they are included in a genealogy, written in a way which indicates that it is God-directed, because of their husbands and the sons they bore to them. They are both women and *mothers*.

In the light of this, it is significant that throughout Mt 1-2 Mary is called either 'woman' (Greek: *hê gunê*: 1:20, 24) or, with remarkably regularity, 'his mother' (Greek: *hê mêtêr autou*: 1:18; 2:11, 13, 14, 20, 21). Behind the presentation of Mary in Mt 1:16 and then, implicitly, throughout Mt 1-2, lies hidden the early Church's growing understanding of Mary as the great woman of faith, laying herself open to the mystery of God's plans for her unique womanly and motherly role. For Matthew and the traditions which stand behind his story of Jesus' birth, Mary's greatness lay in her preparedness to be woman and mother in response to the designs of God, however strange these ways may have appeared to her, to Joseph, the man she loved, and especially to the religious and cultural absolutes of the world in which she lived (1:18-25).[14]

---

[14] This interpretation makes sense of Joseph's anguish (v. 19), an anguish only overcome through his own response in faith (v. 24), as well as the ridicule and public opprobium which have helped to produce 1:18-25. See R. E. Brown, *The Birth of the Messiah*, pp. 142-143. On Christian faith as a questioning of all religious and cultural absolutes, see F. J. Moloney, 'Jesus Christ: The Question to Cultures', *Pacifica* 1 (1988) 15-43. Crucial to vv. 18-25, of course, is Matthew's clear indication that the child is conceived of the Holy Spirit (see 1:19). Mary is a virgin. I will devote more space to this in my consideration of the Lucan material. See below, pp. 16-18.

Chapter 4

The Gospel of Luke:
The Virgin Mother of Jesus
and the First of all Believers

While the Matthean Church's understanding of the role and person of Mary, the woman and mother of Jesus of Nazareth needs to be discovered by seeing her unique place in God's history, standing beside — yet surpassing — other great women and mothers (Mt 1:1-17), in the Gospel of Luke she plays a more prominent role. This is particularly so with the Lucan infancy narrative (Lk 1-2), where she is always at the centre of the story.[1] However, Luke's interest in Mary does not cease there. She appears during the public ministry in 8:19-21 (the Lucan parallel to Mk 3:31-35) and in 11:27-28, where a woman from the crowd sings her praises. Indeed, her story does not conclude until the opening scenes of the Acts of the Apostles, as she gathers with the infant Church in the upper room, awaiting the gift of the Spirit (Acts 1:14).[2]

For the purposes of this study, I will analyse the annunciation scene (1:26-34) in some detail, and then apply the conclusions of that analysis to a more general consideration of the other Lucan Marian material.[3]

The annunciation to Mary

The annunciation scene (1:26-34) must be placed within Luke's overall design for his infancy narrative which can justifiably be described as a story of two infancies.[4] After the prologue (1:1-4) we read two annunciation stories, that of the Baptist (1:5-25) and

---

[1] Contemporary scholarship generally agrees that Luke's Gospel was written for a largely gentile Church some time in the 80's of the first century. See the survey of W. G. Kümmel, *Introduction to the New Testament*, pp. 150-151.

[2] It is almost universally agreed that the Gospel of Luke and the Acts of the Apostles form the two parts of one work from the same author. On this, see W. G. Kümmel, *Introduction to the New Testament*, pp. 156-159.

[3] For a study of all the Lucan Marian material, see F. J. Moloney, *Woman: First among the Faithful*, pp. 40-56.

[4] For a more detailed analysis, see F. J. Moloney, *The Living Voice of the Gospel*, pp. 93-104.

15

that of Jesus (1:26-34). The two mothers, bearing their sons, then meet (1:39-56). Two births and naming follow: the Baptist (1:57-80), and then Jesus (2:1-21). The infant Jesus is then presented in the Temple, to receive the recognition of the Old Testament figures of Simeon and Anna (2:22-40). Finally, the young man, Jesus, announces to his puzzled parents, as they find him in the Temple, that he must concern himself with the affairs of his Father (2:41-52).

It is within this beautifully constructed narrative that Luke uses the Old Testament pattern of an annunciation of a birth to give his readers a powerful introduction to both Jesus and his mother.[5] The scene opens with a deliberate narrative link back to the experience of Elizabeth's hiding herself for *five months* in 1:24. We now read: '*In the sixth month* the angel Gabriel was sent' (1:26). This reference to the sixth month also links with the quickening of the child in Elizabeth's womb in the visitation scene which immediately follows (1:41). The common physical experience of a mother is read by Elizabeth as a salute to the Lord being carried by her young kinswoman.

The angel comes 'to a virgin'. The term *parthenos* appears twice in v. 27. This is significant, as it is Luke's way of indicating that Mary was a virgin at the conception of Jesus. The clear indications of Luke and Matthew in this respect should leave no shadow of doubt that the early Church believed that such was the case.[6] There is a great deal of discussion over the origins and the significance of such a belief.[7] I have no desire to enter into that

---

5 The several annunciations of the infancy narratives (see Mt 1:20-21; Luke 1:11-20, 26-34; 2:9-15) all follow a literary pattern which has its origins in the great annunciations of the Old Testament (Gen 16:7-12 [Ishmael]; 17:1-21 [Isaac]; Judg 13:2-21 [Samson]). On this, see the excellent survey of R. E. Brown, *The Birth of the Messiah*, pp. 292-298.

6 The clarity of Mt 1:16, 18-25 and Luke 1:27, 34-38, along with the strong irony of John 8:41 is sufficient evidence of the early Church's belief in the virginal conception of Jesus. There is no need to attempt, through a strained exegesis of such texts as Gal 4:4, Mk 6:3 and Jn 1:13, to prove something which is made perfectly clear in other texts. J. A. Fitzmyer, 'The Virginal Conception of Jesus in the New Testament', *Theological Studies* 34 (1973) 541-575 gives a good survey, but questions whether it was Luke's intention to indicate this point of view. He has been convincingly answered on this issue by R. E. Brown, 'Luke's Description of the Virginal Conception', *Theological Studies* 35 (1974) 360-362.

7 For the second edition of a classical, and still comprehensive discussion, see J. G. Macken, *The Virgin Birth of Christ* (London: James Clarke, 1958). A more succinct survey can be found in R. E. Brown, *The Birth of the Messiah*, pp. 516-531. An excellent bibliography is provided in *ibid.*, pp. 531-533.

discussion, but I would like to make two points that are often disregarded in the debate.

1. Although the question of Mary's virginity became very important in the later life and preaching of the Church, for the Gospels (Matthew, Luke and John) her physical state at the conception of Jesus is not about the *virtue of Mary* but about the *origins of Jesus*. It expresses a belief that Jesus is 'from God'. Thus, the virginity of Mary, in the New Testament, is not a mariological question, but a Christological issue of considerable importance.[8]

2. What, then, can we say about Mary's being a virgin when called by the angel of the Lord to be the mother of 'the Son of God' (see 1:35)? We must allow Mary herself to tell us what it means. In her *Magnificat* she proclaims: 'He has regarded the low estate of his handmaiden' (1:48). The ancient oriental world generally regarded virginity as sterility. The only value given to a virgin 'was her usefulness as a producer of children, especially sons who could carry on their father's name and give him a continued existence'.[9] The Old Testament reflects that view. Jephthah's daughter bewails her virginity, not the fact that she is about to lose her life (see Judg 11:37-40). Amos and other prophets illustrate the depth of the misery of the chosen people by comparing them to a virgin doomed to die without children (see Amos 5:1-2. See also Hos 1:2-9; 2:4-23; Jer 1:15; 2:13; Joel 1:8). There is no Hebrew word to describe an unmarried man, as such a state was simply unthinkable. Jeremiah is asked to live a celibate life as a prophetic sign, telling of the destruction and desolation of Jerusalem (Jer 16:1-9). So it was with Mary. Her virginity is not a controlling of the impulses of the body in order to rise to divinity. It is an impoverishment, and it brings her scorn from the world (see Mt 1:18-25), but a profound openness to God and to the strangeness of his ways. Leonardo Boff has said it well:

---

[8] For a clearly argued statement of the Christological importance of Mary's virginity, see J. Ratzinger, *Daughter Zion*, pp. 47-61.

[9] O. J. Baab, Art. 'Virgin' in G. A. Buttrick (ed.), *The Interpreter's Dictionary of the Bible* (New York/Nashville: Abingdon Press, 1962) Vol. 4, pp. 787-788. The quotation comes from p. 787. See also, H.-U. von Balthasar, *Mary for Today* (Slough: St Paul Publications, 1987) pp. 47-50.

Mary's biological virginity is part of the structure of the *kenosis*, the self-emptying, with all its attendant humiliations, that she shares with her Son. Her biological virginity is lowliness and deprivation, as far as others can see. It has value neither in society nor for religion. But Mary makes this situation of an apparently mean existential condition the path of humility, serene surrender and boundless trust in God. She aspires to nothing. She is only completely available. It is this attitude that allows God to be born of her, first in her heart, and then in her most pure womb.[10]

She is then further described as 'betrothed to a man whose name was Joseph' (v. 27). This affirmation must be taken seriously. As yet, Mary has not been led to the house of Joseph, but her being betrothed to a man explicitly named as 'of the house of David' already makes her his 'wife' (*hê gunê*: see Mt 1.20).[11] She too belongs to that house. Whatever the later apocryphal gospels may have made of this relationship, there are no indications in the Lucan text of any vow to perpetual virginity.[12]

The Old Testament pattern of a birth narrative begins as Gabriel greets the young woman with an expression that is difficult to render precisely: *chairê kecharitomênê*. A tone of joy underlies both of these verbs, which come from the same basic root.[13] One greets Mary, and the other is used in a perfect passive form to describe her as one to whom God has freely given his gifts: 'Rejoice, O highly favoured one!'. Here Luke is striking a theme that is central to his account: the absolute initiative of God in all that is happening. God did not *have* to choose Mary — he chose one of us out of

---

[10] L. Boff, *The Maternal Face of God. The Feminine and Its Religious Expressions* (San Francisco: Harper & Row, 1987) p. 139. On this see, see pp. 137-139. See also H.-U. von Balthasar, *Mary for Today*, pp. 57-64. Mary is thus the personification of one of Luke's major interests: the poor, the rejected and the outcasts of society. For a survey, see F. Bovon, *Luc le théologien. Vingt-cinq ans de recherche (1950-1975)* (Neuchatel: Delachaux et Niestlé, 1978) pp. 410-415. For a detailed study, see L. T. Johnson, *The Literary Function of Possessions in Luke-Acts* (SBL Dissertation Series 39; Missoula: Scholars Press, 1977).

[11] See R. E. Brown, *The Birth of the Messiah*, pp. 123-124 for a synthesis of these practices. For more detail, see J. Jeremias, *Jerusalem in the Time of Jesus* (London: SCM Press, 1969) pp. 364-368.

[12] For a summary of the apocryphal legends, and some of the European art which such legends have inspired, see A. Horton, *The Child Jesus* (London: Geoffrey Chapman, 1975) pp. 36-75. See also R. E. Brown et alii (eds.), *Mary in the New Testament*, pp. 243-253, 257-270.

[13] See X. Jacques, *List of New Testament Words Sharing Common Elements* (Rome: Biblical Institute Press, 1969) p. 120.

his incredible freedom and love. This is what Mary recognises in her *Magnificat* (see especially 1:48-49).[14]

Once this is clear, then we are able better to understand the power of the angel's following affirmation: 'The Lord is with you'. This expression, taken from the Old Testament (see Gen 26:24; 28:15; Ex 3:12; Judg 6:12; Jer 1:8, 19; 15:20),[15] is an assurance that no matter what might befall her, and no matter what might be thought or said of her, God's plans for her will be effectively realised. 'This expression *does not define a static presence, but a dynamic power* --- The saying 'the Lord is with thee' takes away fear and gives strength; its effect is blessing for Mary, the people, the world'.[16] However, Mary must be seen as free to respond or not to respond to this initiative of God.

Although Luke is following the Old Testament pattern, Mary's being troubled and 'considering in her mind what sort of greeting this might be' (v. 29) is understandable. Notice that Mary's *first* reaction is one of human puzzlement and confusion. She is unable to utter a single word in her shock and consternation. Thus, the angel, following the annunciation literary pattern, calms her fears and explains further: 'You have found favour with God' (v. 30). Again we find Luke using an Old Testament expression which always indicates the free and gracious choice of Yahweh, who favours particular women and men (see, for example, Gen 6:8; Judg 6:17; I Sam 1:18; II Sam 15:25). The stress is still upon the mystery of a God who chooses one of us.

In vv. 31-33 the literary pattern continues with the annunciation of the conception and birth of a son, his name Jesus, and a description of the child. Notice that at this stage nothing has been said of the nature of the conception. In fact, in this first part of the actual annunciation and description of the child, he is described in a way which reflects the classical terms of Jewish messianic hopes:

---

[14] This important point has been well made by *Lumen Gentium* 60: 'The Blessed Virgin's salutary influence on men (and women) *originates not in any inner necessity but in the disposition of God.* It flows forth from the superabundance of the merits of Christ, rests on his mediation and draws all its power from it' (Stress and parenthesis mine). See also *Redemptoris Mater,* 38-41.

[15] See W. C. van Unnik, '*Dominus Vobiscum:* The Background of a Liturgical Formula', in *New Testament Essays. Studies in Memory of Thomas Walter Manson 1893-1958* (Manchester: University Press, 1959) pp. 276-286 for a list of Old Testament and Jewish sources where the expression is used. The article runs from pp. 270-305.

[16] *Ibid.,* pp. 276 & 289.

He will be called great,
and he will be called
the son of the Most High;
and the Lord God will give to him
the throne of his father David,
and he will reign over the house of Jacob forever;
and of his kingdom there will be no end (vv. 32-33).

The child is described as the son of the Most High and the son of David; Mary is told that he will be great, that he will reign over the house of David forever and that his kingdom will have no end. *All* of these expectations can be found in the Jewish hopes for their coming Messiah, including 'the son of the Most High'.[17] Mary is being told that she will be the mother of the expected Messiah. Although an extraordinary privilege is being bestowed upon her through the initiative of God, in the context of the feverish messianic expectation of the first century, she is within the realms of the *expected* and the *humanly possible*.

It is precisely this 'possibility' which Mary questions in v. 34. Her question will lead to a further revelation that this child will be someone who surpasses all contemporary Jewish messianic hopes. It is important to notice, however, that while Luke is using the literary pattern of an annunciation gradually to reveal the full significance of Jesus, he is also showing his readers a journey of faith on the part of Mary, his mother-to-be. While the greeting of the angel led to puzzlement and fear (v. 29), Mary now poses a perfectly reasonable question. She has moved from *astonishment* to *reason*. Just as Zechariah asked for some explanation of *how* Elizabeth could conceive a child, given her age (1:18), so also Mary asks *how* she can conceive, given her physical situation: 'How can this be, *since I am not knowing a man*' (v. 34). I have given a very literal translation (Greek: *epei andra ou ginôskô*) to avoid any confusion. The use of the verb *ginôskein* indicates that Mary is referring to the sexual union (see Gen 4:1; 19:8; Judg 11:39; 21:12; I Sam 1:19 etc.).

---

[17] See, on this, H. Cazelles, *Le Messie de la Bible* (Série Jésus et Jésus Christ; Paris: Desclée, 1978). On the Jewish use of 'son of the Most High' as a messianic term (based on Ps 2:7 and II Sam 7:14), see B. J. Byrne, *'Sons of God – Seed of Abraham.' A Study of the Sonship of God of all Christians in Paul against the Jewish Background* (Analecta Biblica 83; Rome: Biblical Institute Press, 1979) pp. 9-78.

The present tense of the verb shows that Mary recognises the crucial importance of her decision in this encounter. At this moment she is a virgin, and does not have a sexual relationship with Joseph. How can it be that she will conceive a child? Some scholars have argued that Mary's query in v. 34 indicates her prior decision to remain a virgin.[18] Apart from the strain that such an interpretation puts on the present tense of the verb, it makes little sense of the context. What is the point of the betrothal in v. 27 if Mary has decided that she will remain a virgin? Whatever may have in fact been the nature of the relationship between Mary and Joseph after the birth of Jesus and however well the Fathers of the Church may have spoken properly of Mary's perpetual virginity,[19] that is a later (and justifiable) point of view. We must allow Luke's Gospel to tell its own story, and not impose these later developments upon his narrative.

Basic to the structure of this account, as I have been indicating throughout, is the literary pattern of an annunciation of birth. Following that pattern, Mary has reacted with a query. I have further suggested, however, that Luke uses the pattern to show a development in her reaction to the revelation of God. She has now moved from her first reaction of confusion (v. 29) to reason and logic (v. 34). Luke uses this second reaction to indicate the all important message of the nature of this conception: there is to be no human father!

---

[18] There are several variations in this argument, and most scholars have abandoned attempts to identify in 1:34 the indications of a *vow* to perpetual virginity. But to read the passage as a decision to live as a virgin, they must read into the present tense 'I am not knowing' some form of a future expression 'I will not know'. See, for example, G. Graystone, *Virgin of all Virgins: The Interpretation of Luke 1:34* (Rome: Pio X, 1968); J. McHugh, *The Mother of Jesus in the New Testament*, pp. 193-199; M. Miguens, *The Virgin Birth*, pp. 77-82. For an excellent survey of the contemporary discussion, see A. Serra, Art. 'Vergine' in S. De Fiores – S. Meo (eds.), *Nuovo Dizionario di Mariologia*, pp. 1437-1445.

[19] Notably by Augustine, *De Sancta Virginitate* 4,4; PL 60:308, where Lk 1:34 is explicitly discussed, but widely defended by Origen, Ambrose, John Chrysostom, Ephraem, Gregory of Nyssa and Jerome. The Lateran Synod of 649, building on the Council of Constantinople (553) introduced the formula 'virginity before, in and after giving birth'. On this, see the study of M. Schmaus, Art. 'Mariology', in A. Darlap (ed.), *Sacramentum Mundi. An Encyclopaedia of Theology* (London: Burns & Oates, 1968) Vol. 3, pp. 376-383 and G. Söll, *Storia dei Dogmi Mariani*, pp. 173-225. See also the comprehensive and well documented survey of S. De Fiores, Art. 'Vergine', in S. De Fiores – S. Meo (eds.), *Nuovo Dizionario di Mariologia*, pp. 1454-1473. See also R. E. Brown et alii (eds.), *Mary in the New Testament*, pp. 270-282.

While vv. 32-33 spoke of a messianic king, v. 35 speaks of the conception and the child in a way which surpasses all Jewish religious and cultural expectations:

The Holy Spirit will come upon you,
and the power of the Most High will overshadow you;
therefore the child to be born will be called holy,
the Son of God (v. 35).

Still following the annunciation pattern the *sign* of Elizabeth is given (v. 36). If Mary is faced with a promise that she will be the virgin mother of the Son of God which she could regard as *impossible*, then the sign given to her is the maternity of her elderly kinswoman – a further *impossibility*. In explanation of what is happening to *both* women, the angel announces in v. 37: 'For with God nothing will be impossible'.

Notice how carefully Luke has linked both annunciation scenes. Both maternities are impossible. All that we have read in 1:5-36 is quite impossible, yet with God nothing is impossible. Luke's central idea remains that of the absolute initiative, freedom, and overpowering goodness of God. The text is not *primarily* about Mary, but about the transforming power of a great and loving God who can raise up the lowly (see 1:51-52). Now the indications of the earlier moments of the angel's encounter with Mary become fully explicit. The ultimate reason for all the incredible promises which have been made is God, and 'with God nothing is impossible' (v. 37).

It is the response of Mary to this God which gives her a special place in the story of God's action in the history of women and men:

Behold I am the handmaid of the Lord;
let it be done to me
according to your word (v. 38).

The appearance of the angel has led to an amazed puzzlement (v. 29); the annunciation of the birth of the long-awaited Messiah has led to a perfectly logical objection (v. 34). Now Mary is aware that she has been caught up into a plan of God that reaches outside all human measurement and control. She is being asked to give herself and her future history to 'the Holy Spirit ... the power of the Most High'. She *could* have remained in the realm of the controllable, and baulked at such a suggestion.[20] Instead she commits herself to the ways of God in a consummate act of faith (v. 38). Luke has shown us a further moment in the early Church's growing understanding of the person and the role of Mary: she is a *woman* who was called to be the *virgin mother* of Jesus. Her acceptance of that consummate vocation makes her – in Luke's story line – the first person to risk everything for the sake of Jesus Christ: the first of all believers.

During Luke's version of the public ministry of Jesus we find that this Evangelist reshapes the rather negative tone of Mk 3:31-35 to continue his presentation of Mary, the mother of Jesus who – more than anyone else – is the one who hears the word of God and lives by it (1:38). Luke reports:

> Then his mother and his brothers came to him, but they could not reach him for the crowd. And he was told, 'Your mother and your brothers are standing outside, desiring to see you'. But he said to them, 'My mother and my brothers are those who hear the word of God and do it' (8:19-21).

Gone is the Marcan contrast between 'outside' and 'inside', between human family and the new family of faith.[21] For Luke, Mary is the one, *par excellence*, who hears the word and does it. Her association with Jesus began in this way in 1:26-38, and it continues during his public ministry.

'She treasured these things in her heart'

There is a further feature of the Lucan infancy narrative which merits our attention. On two occasions we are told that Mary, the mother of Jesus kept or treasured all these things in her heart (2:19, 51). These expressions are sometimes taken as an indication of certain 'family secrets', such as the virginal life of Mary which only Mary and Joseph could possibly know. For scholars trying to

---

[20] See, on this, M. B. Pennington, *Mary Today*, pp. 7-17. My argument could be countered by the objection that such a refusal was impossible because of the Immaculate Conception. Here my introductory remarks (see above, pp. 1-3) are important. Luke's Gospel was written in the 80's of the first century. After centuries of debate, the Immaculate Conception was eventually defined in 1854! We must allow Luke to tell the story in his way. The truth of the dogma of the Immaculate Conception is not at stake. It is simply that Luke cannot be asked to be aware of something which the Church herself took almost 2000 years to appreciate.

[21] See above, p. 6.

establish a firm historical basis for such difficult and private issues as a virginal conception, these expressions are used as proof that Mary did have treasured secrets, but that she communicated them.[22]

This search for the brute facts of history misses an important Lucan contribution to the developing Marian reflection of the early Church. What must be noticed is that in all the contexts where the expression 'to treasure in the heart' is mentioned, there are also indications that Mary did not fully understand what was happening to her, or to her son. The whole context of the birth story (2:1-21) – so full of extraordinary signs and events – creates wonder and often puzzlement, but not understanding. The Evangelist informs his readers of the parents' reaction to their son's sharp rebuke in the Temple: 'And they did not understand the saying which he spoke to them' (2:50). A similar puzzlement is found in the scene of the presentation of Jesus in the Temple: 'And his mother and father marvelled at what was said about him' (2:33). It is here that we find a major clue to the true meaning of Mary's treasuring in the heart.

The expression is closely linked to an Old Testament phrase, found in the various books of the Bible (see, for example, Gen 37:11; I Sam 2:13; Mal 2:2) but becoming more important in the wisdom literature (see, for example Sir 39:1-3; Prov 31; Ps 119:11) and the apocalyptic literature (see, for example, Dan 1:8; 4:28; 7:28).[23]

In these passages a human has been the recipient of some form of revelation from God. The experience of this revelation is beyond the understanding of the recipient. There is a mystery about the revelation whose significance he or she cannot fully grasp. In such a situation one can simply marvel, and then go one's way (see, for example Lk 2:18),[24] or one can 'treasure in the heart'. The mystery can be taken into the deepest recesses of one's being, guarded and pondered over in one's heart. The faithful ones simply await God's time and plan for the full revelation of the mysteries entrusted to them.

---

[22] See, for example, J. McHugh, *The Mother of Jesus in the New Testament*, pp. 147-149; M. Miguens, *The Virgin Birth*, pp. 128-132.

[23] See R. E. Brown, *The Birth of the Messiah*, pp. 429-431.

[24] In fact, this group, described as 'those who heard', make a wrong choice. In 1:66 they 'treasured in their hearts' the events surrounding the birth of the Baptist, but the same group simply 'wonders' at the birth of Jesus in 2:18.

This is Mary's situation. An angel from heaven has appeared to her, telling her that she is to become the virginal mother of the Son of God through the overshadowing of the Holy Spirit. Shepherds have come in from the fields with a message of heavenly revelations from angelic choirs. As we have already seen, all of this was well beyond anything Mary could hope fully to understand or control: 'How can this be?' (1:34). The same perplexity is there in both the presentation of the infant Jesus and the finding of the boy Jesus in the Temple (2:33, 50). *Never* in these accounts is Mary in control. In faith, she treasures all that has been revealed to her, as she awaits the fulness of God's revelation to her.

Hans-Urs von Balthasar, in a context dealing with Mary's living by faith, led by the Spirit towards the foundation of the Church, describes her situation as follows:

> In no way at all does she understand everything completely from the first moment onwards but has to work away tirelessly in order to understand all these overpowering ideas as well as she may. For this she has one basic experience: she was told that she would conceive a son not by a man but by the Holy Spirit. And behold, she, the virgin, conceived. And this son was described to her as 'Son of the Most High' (Lk 1:32). How was a Jewess to understand that Yahweh had a son? But the fact of her pregnancy was there. The incarnation was a fact on which she was continually to ponder without comprehending it.[25]

Mary is a woman and a virgin mother called to a unique greatness. She could not possibly be expected to understand the depths of the mysteries into which she had been drawn through her unconditional assent to the ways of God in her life: she was to be the giver of the flesh and blood in the mystery of the Incarnation. How this could be and why it should happen to her, she could not understand. But as mother of all believers – of all those who would attempt to respond to God in this way – she was the first and most perfect of those who simply 'treasure all these things in their hearts'.

Another passage from the Lucan infancy stories where this same theme can be found is 2:34-35: 'Behold this child is set for the fall and rising of many in Israel, and for a sign that is spoken against

[25] H.-U. von Balthasar, *Mary for Today*, pp. 34-35. I would argue that 'son of the Most High' in 1:32 was comprehensible, but not 'Son of God' in 1:35. See above, pp. 19-20.

– and a sword will pierce your own soul also – that thoughts out of many hearts may be revealed'. What is to be made of this reference to a sword which would pass through the heart of Mary? It is inserted as a parenthesis within a context dealing with Jesus' being the revelation of the reigning presence of God which would be refused and accepted in Israel.[26]

The whole passage reflects Luke's overall presentation of the preaching of Jesus, and then of the early Church as described in the Acts of the Apostles, rejected by Israel. The placing of the word 'fall' first indicates that while there may have been Jews who accepted Jesus, the majority refused to listen. Within this context, Mary is presented as a part of this experience, but a different image is used. No longer does Luke speak of 'falling and rising', but of a piercing of her soul with a sword. However, she is carefully linked with Israel's experience of falling or rising by the word 'also': 'And a sword will pierce your own soul *also*'.[27]

The figure of a sword piercing is found in Ezek 14:17, where the image is used for the judgment of the Lord passing through the land. The sword is not one of punishment, but of discrimination, destroying some and sparing others, depending upon their response to the word of God (see also Ezek 5:1-2; 6:8-9; 12:14-16; Is 49:1-2). This is the background for Simeon's parenthetic remark to Mary. The whole context speaks of Jesus' causing the fall and the rising of many in Israel ... and among the Israelites stands his own mother! As Simeon tells her of the crucial role her son will play in the history of her people's response to God, he adds that she is to be included with all her people: she also will still be called to further decisions.

However, while Simeon's words emphasise the 'fall' of many in Israel, such is not the case for the mother of Jesus. While she forms a part of Israel, and therefore must experience the discriminatory presence of the sword which her son will bring among her people

---

[26] Naturally, the reference to a sword passing through the heart of Mary – as well as being the basis for some rather gruesome and fantastic statues – has created difficulties and discussion from the patristic period onward. For a survey of interpretations, see R. E. Brown, *The Birth of the Messiah*, pp. 462-463.

[27] The Greek expression *de* which I have translated as 'also' (along with the RSV) is disputed by textual critics. The manuscript evidence is finely balanced, and the context leads me to urge its inclusion.

(see Mt 10:34-36),[28] she cannot simply be included with the rest of her people. The parenthesis is added to Simeon's words because while Mary cannot be spared the destiny of all her people, she is not destined to fall. Being an Israelite does not guarantee salvation . . . nor does being a member of his family. Only a never-failing openness to the strangeness of his ways effects such a guarantee, and Mary has already demonstrated such openness (see especially 1:26-38).

At this stage of Luke's narrative, however, Mary's journey of faith is just beginning. It is along this journey of faith, where her initial decision (see 1:38) must be repeated over and over again, without ever fully understanding the mysteries to which she is responding, that Mary will experience a sword piercing her soul.

The Evangelist Luke speaks to readers who know that, while she cannot be spared the sword of discrimination, she will decide positively. From the perspective of the Evangelist and his communities, the journey of Mary has come to its end,[29] but Luke inserts this parenthesis into the prophecy of Simeon to instruct his readers that Mary's *Fiat* did not lift her out of the necessary puzzlement, anxiety and pain which often arises from the radical nature of the Christian vocation. Despite her remarkable initiation into the Christian mystery, she still had to proceed through the rest of her life, 'treasuring in her heart' the mysteries revealed to her, never fully understanding, but patiently waiting for God's time and God's ultimate answer.

Mary and the disciples

There are two further passages from Luke-Acts where Mary appears. Only Mary is found in the infancy narratives (Lk 1-2),

---

[28] This passage from Matthew was probably drawn from the Q source, common to Matthew and Luke: 'Do not think that I have come to bring peace on earth. I have not come to bring peace *but a sword*'. Luke does not use this passage, but my interpretation of Luke 2:35a would show that he uses 'the sword' with the same meaning in that passage. See R. E. Brown, *The Birth of the Messiah*, p. 464.

[29] Although we have no proof one way or the other, I suspect that Mary does not form a part of the Lucan community itself, and that she is already deceased. Luke has elevated her into such a significant role as mother, woman and perfect disciple, that she has now become more than just a historical person to whom her fellow Christians can look for instruction. She is a 'symbol' of all that God can do for those who are unreservedly receptive to his word (see 1:38).

in the public ministry (8:19-21) . . . and with the disciples in the
upper room in the earliest days of the Christian Church (Acts 1:14).

But Luke reports another occasion during the public ministry
when Mary, although not reported as present, is called into question
by a woman from the crowd:

> And it happened while he was saying these things that a woman
> from the crowd, raising her voice, said to him, 'Blessed is the womb
> that bore you, and the breasts you sucked'. But he said, 'No, blessed
> are those who hear the word of God and keep it' (11:27-28).

In many ways this passage serves as a warning for all subsequent
interpretation of the greatness of Mary. Her greatness does not lie
in her physical privileges, although that is where a great deal of
our attention has been directed. Her greatness, her blessedness lies
in her unconditional assent — in both word and deed — to God's
gifts to her.

St Augustine has left us a famous eloquent interpretation of this
passage:

> Indeed and indeed she did the Father's will and it is a greater thing
> for her that she was Christ's disciple than that she was his mother.
> It is a happier thing to be his disciple than to be his mother. Blessed
> then is Mary who bore her Lord in her body before she gave him
> birth.
>
> See if it isn't as I say. The Lord was journeying on and the crowds
> were following him. He did a work of divine power and this woman
> in the crowd cried out: 'Blessed is the womb that bore you and
> the breasts that you sucked.' But they must not think that blessed-
> ness lay in bodily relationship, so what did the Lord answer?
> 'Blessed rather are those who hear the word of God and keep it.'
> Therefore Mary is blessed because she 'heard the word of God and
> kept it'. Her mind was filled more fully with Truth than her womb
> by his flesh. Christ is the truth, Christ is made flesh: Christ the
> truth is in Mary's mind, Christ made flesh is in her womb. Greater
> is that which is in her mind than that which she carried in her
> womb.[30]

---

[30] *Sermo* 25,7-8. The Latin text of this sermon (with an Italian translation) can be found
in *Nuova Biblioteca Agostiniana* 30 (1983) 468-479. On this whole theme, see J. Pintard,
'Le principe "prius mente quam corpore . . ." dans la patristique et la théologie latine',
Bulletin de la Societe Francaise d'Etudes Mariales 27 (1970) 25-58. This passage has
unfortunately been interpreted in the opposite direction in *Redemptoris Mater* 20. For
a study of Augustinian Mariology and a collection of the most important texts, see
M. Pellegrino (ed.), *S. Agostino D'Ippona: La Vergine Maria* (Milan: Edizioni Paoline,

Mary's final appearance is in the upper room with the infant Church: 'All these with one accord devoted themselves to prayer, together with Mary the mother of Jesus' (Acts 1:14). In Luke 1-2 she became the first and most wonderful of all believers. During the public life of Jesus (8:19-21 and 11:27-28) she is still there: the one who hears the word of God and keeps it. Both of these passages, as St Augustine has so powerfully indicated, use Jesus' mother to show what it means to *belong* to Jesus, to be one with the Truth: 'It is a happier thing to be his disciple than to be his mother'. For Luke, Mary is clearly the first and the best of all disciples.

But at the beginning of Luke's story of the Church he seems to take his reflections on Mary, the mother of Jesus, a small but important step further. I would suggest that here we find the first hints that this primacy of faith which Mary of Nazareth had so clearly demonstrated, placed her in a special position in the earliest community. As they await the gift from on high, 'the mother of Jesus' is with them. Why does Luke single out this 'woman', the 'mother of Jesus' in such a way?

It appears to me that we have in Acts 1:14 the first indication of an intuition of the earliest Church, reflected in Luke's *Acts of the Apostles* for the first time in a *written* document, which the Fourth Evangelist will carry further and make explicit. The 'woman' and the 'mother of Jesus' (Jn 2:1-11) becomes 'the mother of the disciple' and the 'mother of the Church' (19:25-27).[31]

1987). This extremely rich book is introduced by a fine study from Cardinal Pellegrino: 'Maria SS. nel Pensiero di S. Agostino' (pp. 15-40). As I have already mentioned, the famous passage which I have cited is only one of many passages on Mary from Augustine. One can find other passages which take quite a different direction. However, he is consistent in his interpretation of Lk 11:27-28. See also the reflections of M. B. Pennington, *Mary Today*, pp. 17-20.

[31] See *Redemptoris Mater* 25-28 which uses Acts 1:14 for a reflection along these lines.

Chapter 5

The Fourth Gospel:
Woman and Mother

One of the remarkable features of the Marian material in the Fourth Gospel is that the mother of Jesus is never called 'Mary'. She is called either 'woman' (2:4; 19:16) or 'the mother of Jesus' (2:1, 3, 5; 19:25, 26). There are two places in the Gospel where she plays a most important role — both in terms of John's story, and in terms of the theological message which he is attempting to communicate through the story — where these two expressions are used to speak of her: the account of the first miracle at Cana (John 2:1-11) and the famous scene at the foot of the Cross (19:25-27).[1]

---

[1] Readers familiar with contemporary Johannine scholarship will have noticed that I am not accepting a Johannine indication of the virgin birth in a singular reading of John 1:13: '*He who was born*, not of blood, nor of the will of the flesh nor of the will of man'. This reading has no support in the Greek manuscripts, but is found in several early Latin witnesses: Vetus Latina, Latin Irenaeus, Tertullian, Latin Origen, Ambrose, Augustine, Pseudo Athanasius. A number of modern scholars, and *The Jerusalem Bible* (1966 edition), have accepted it. For detail, see B. M. Metzger, *A Textual Commentary on the Greek New Testament* (London/New York: United Bible Societies, 1971) pp. 196-197. Since 1978 a sophisticated textual, structural and theological argument in defence of the singular reading has been developed, particularly by Ignace de la Potterie in Rome. See especially, I. de la Potterie, 'La Mère de Jésus et la conception virginale du Fils de Dieu', *Marianum* 40 (1978) 41-90; Idem, 'Il parto verginale del Verbo incarnato: 'Non ex sanguinibus ... sed ex Deo natus est' (Gv. 1,13)', *Marianum* 45 (1983) 127-174; P. Hofrichter, *Nicht aus Blut sondern monogen aus Gott geboren. Textkritische, dogmengeschichtliche und exegetische Untersuchung zu Joh 1,13-14* (Forschung zur Bibel 31; Stuttgart: Katholisches Bibelwerk, 1978); M. Vellanickal, *The Divine Sonship of Christians in the Johannine Writings* (Analecta Biblica 72; Rome: Biblical Institute Press, 1977) pp. 105-161. For full bibliographical references to the discussion, see I. de la Potterie, 'Il parto verginale . . .', pp. 127-130 and A. Serra, Art. 'Vergine', in S. De Fiores – S. Meo, *Nuovo Dizionario di Mariologia*, pp. 1445-1448. On textual grounds, apart from the overwhelming evidence of the Greek uncials, I find it difficult to accept that the third and fourth century manuscript tradition would have deliberately *eliminated* an original reference to the virginity of Mary, but easy to accept that the early Latin Fathers might have *introduced* it (especially Tertullian!). As well as finding in 1:13 a Gospel reference to the later doctrine of 'virginitas in partu', theologically de la Potterie stresses the important Johannine theme that Jesus is the visible incarnation of God. While this is true for the Fourth Gospel, it appears to me that we need to look at the rest of the Marian material for guidance. De la Potterie and his followers have not paid sufficient attention to the womanly and maternal aspects of the Johannine Marian teaching present in all Johannine Marian

It is fascinating that 'woman' and 'mother', the terms which were used at the very beginnings of the written traditions of the Christian Church (Gal 4:4 and Mk 3:31-35; 6:1-6a), are found again at the end of that inspired tradition.[2] Equally fascinating, it appears to me, is the use of the term 'woman' in the image which dominates the instruction given to the disciples in 16:21-24. This has been little used in New Testament reflections on Mary, but it merits some closer attention.[3]

The miracle at Cana

There is every indication that the section of the Fourth Gospel which runs from 2:1 to 4:54 has been constructed by the Evangelist to teach his readers the nature of authentic faith.[4] An important element in this scheme is the literary frame around the narrative: the two Cana miracles (2:1-11 and 4:46-54). The interpretation of the first miracle at Cana has fascinated many scholars, and here

---

material, but not found in 1:13. I do believe that the Fourth Evangelist knew and accepted the tradition of the virgin birth, and that it lies behind the irony of 8:41. See Paul D. Duke, *Irony in the Fourth Gospel* (Atlanta: John Knox Press, 1985) p. 76.

[2] See above, pp. 5-8. I am taking it for granted that the Fourth Gospel was one of the most recent pieces of literature in the New Testament. No doubt the Johannine community and its literature had a long history (we possess a Gospel and three letters from the same community), but it seems to me that it appeared in its final form about 100 A.D. On these issues, see F. J. Moloney, 'Revisiting John', *Scripture Bulletin* 11 (Summer 1980) pp. 9-15; Idem, *The Word Became Flesh* (Theology Today Series 14; Dublin/Cork: Mercier Press, 1977) pp. 9-26. See also, R. E. Brown, *The Community of the Beloved Disciple. The Life, Loves, and Hates of an Individual Church in New Testament Times* (London: Geoffrey Chapman, 1979).

[3] Rupert von Deutz used the text in reference to Mary, and linked it with 19:25-27. See *In Johannem XIII*; PL 169, 789c-790c. Among modern scholars, attention has been drawn to the possible Marian interpretation by A. Feuillet, 'L'heure de la femme (Jn 16:21) et l'heure de la Mère de Jésus', *Biblica* 47 (1966) 168-184, 361-370, 557-573; Idem, *Jésus et sa Mère d'après les récits lucaniens de l'enfance et d'après saint Jean* (Paris: Gabalda, 1974) pp. 134-139. My attention was drawn to the further possible Marian implications of this passage by a footnote in a splendid work devoted to the structure and interpretation of Jn 13:1 – 17:26. See Y. Simoens, *La gloire d'aimer. Structures stylistiques et interprétatives dans le Discours de la Cène (Jn 13-17)* (Analecta Biblica 90; Rome: Biblical Institute Press, 1981) p. 165, note 14.

[4] For the detailed argumentation of this case, see F. J. Moloney, 'From Cana to Cana (Jn 2:1 – 4:54) and the Fourth Evangelist's Concept of Correct (and Incorrect) Faith', *Salesianum* 40 (1978) 817-843. It has also been reproduced in E. A. Livingstone (ed.), *Studia Biblica II. Papers on the Gospels. Sixth International Congress on Biblical Studies. Oxford 3-7 April 1978* (Sheffield: JSOT Press, 1980) pp. 185-213. A simplified version can be found in F. J. Moloney, *The Living Voice of the Gospel*, pp. 211-219.

I will only indicate a few features, especially those concerned with the overall argument of my study.[5]

There is a very interesting parallel between the two Cana miracles which throws into relief the Johannine interest in the question of true faith. Breaking all the form critical rules for the telling of a miracle story,[6] John constructs *both* stories along exactly the same lines:

2:1-11	4:46-54
1. *Problem:* The wine failed (v. 3).	1. *Problem:* An official whose son was ill (v. 46).
2. *Request:* The *mother* of Jesus said to him, 'They have no wine' (v. 3).	2. *Request:* He went down and begged him to come and heal his son (v. 47).
3. *Rebuke:* 'O *woman,* what have you to do with me?' (v. 4).	3. *Rebuke:* 'Unless you see signs and wonders you will not believe!' (v. 48).
4. *Reaction:* His *mother* said to the servants, 'Do whatever he tells (Greek: *legein*) you' (v. 5).	4. *Reaction:* 'Go your son will live'. The man believed the word (Greek: *logos*) that Jesus spoke to him (v. 50).
5. *Consequence:* A miracle which leads to the faith of others (disciples) (vv. 6-11).	5. *Consequence:* A miracle which leads to the faith of others (household) (vv. 51-53).

Both scenes are rounded off with a comment from the Evangelist which shows he is anxious that his reader notice that these two accounts of miracles performed at Cana are a statement and a re-statement of the same themes:

2:11: This, the *first of his signs, Jesus did* at Cana in *Galilee.*	4:54: This was now the *second sign which Jesus did* when he had come from Judea to *Galilee.*

---

5   For some indication of the widespread scholarly interest in John 2:1-11, see the rich biblio-graphical indications – limited to the Marian interpretation of the passage – in A. Serra, Art. 'Bibbia', in S. De Fiores – S. Meo, *Nuovo Dizionario di Mariologia*, pp. 309-310.

6   For a summary of these 'rules' and the various history of religion parallels which have helped the form critics to establish them, see W. Barclay, *The Gospels and Acts* (London: SCM Press, 1976) Vol. I, pp. 33-41.

This form of construction is called an *inclusion* by the literary critics. It is a method used by both ancient and modern authors to frame a passage in such a way as to make clear to the reader the overarching theme of the whole passage. The message of the whole of John 2:1 – 4:54 must be read in the light of the two examples of perfect faith provided by the mother of Jesus (2:1-11) and the royal official (4:46-54) in the literary 'frames' which begin and end this section of John's narrative.

While there are various stages of faith exhibited by the people in the rest of this part of the Gospel ('the Jews', Nicodemus, John the Baptist, the Samaritan woman and the Samaritan villagers), both the mother of Jesus and the royal official indicate a quality of trust in the word of Jesus which can only be seen as perfect expressions of their faith.

In the two Cana miracles, in the first instance, both the mother of Jesus and the royal official turn to Jesus in trust, but are severely rebuked. However, despite the rebuke, they show that they are not seeking 'signs and wonders' (see 4:48) for their own sake. They show total and unswerving trust in the efficacy of *the word of Jesus* (see 2:5; 4:50). It is for this reason that the mother of Jesus tells the servants to do whatever he *tells* them to do, and it is for the same reason that once Jesus pronounces that his son will live, the royal official believes *the word* of Jesus and goes his way. John has chosen to use the words *legein* and *logos*, because they both come from the same basic root associated with speaking, speech and the word.[7]

A more detailed study of the whole of 2:1 – 4:54 would show that John is most concerned to indicate to his readers the quality of true faith.[8] Throughout the whole of 1:19-51 his first disciples have stumbled towards true faith in a series of confessions: Christ, Elijah, the prophet (see vv. 20-21; 25-27), the Messiah, which means the Christ (v. 41), him of whom Moses in the Law and also the prophets wrote (v. 45), Rabbi, son of God, King of Israel (v. 49). While there is nothing wrong with any of these hopes – they are not enough. He responds to these first stammers of faith with a rebuke and a promise:

---

[7]   See X. Jacques, *List of New Testament Words Sharing Common Elements*, pp. 66-67.
[8]   On this, see F. J. Moloney, 'From Cana to Cana . . ', pp. 827-839 (or pp. 191-199). See above, note 4.

'Because I said to you I saw you under the fig tree do you believe? You shall see greater things than these'. And he said to him, 'Truly, truly, I say to you, you will see heaven opened, and the angels of God ascending and descending upon the Son of man' (1:50-51).[9]

True sight – true belief – must go beyond all their most exalted hopes. Jesus reveals God himself, and the only way to respond to such a revelation, to such a *Word*, is to lay aside all pretensions and commit oneself to it unconditionally.

To commit oneself to 'the word of Jesus', however, does not simply mean to give intellectual assent to everything that he 'says'. One must be prepared to compromise oneself for the whole event of Jesus himself, as the unique once-and-for-all revealing Son of God. The reader is already well aware from the prologue to the Gospel (1:1-18) that Jesus not only 'speaks' the Word, but he 'is' the Word (see 1:1-2, 14).

Appropriate to this aspect of the Johannine Jesus and the Christian response, exemplified in the mother of Jesus and the royal official, are the words of St Ignatius of Antioch:

No doubt it is a fine thing to instruct others, but only if the speaker practises what he preaches. One such teacher there is: 'He who spoke the word, and it was done', and what he achieved even by his silences was well worthy of the Father. One who has truly mastered the utterances of Jesus will . . . thus reach full spiritual maturity (*Ephesians* 15:1-2).[10]

The mother of Jesus and the royal official have made this act of authentic faith in the Word in the two Cana miracles; they are portrayed by the Fourth Evangelist as having come to 'full spiritual maturity'.

While there is unquestionably a close literary and theological parallel between the mother of Jesus and the royal official, there are three very important points about the total commitment in faith of the mother of Jesus which merit special attention.

9   For a more detailed analysis of 1:19-51, see F. J. Moloney, *The Living Voice of the Gospel*, pp. 203-210. For 1:51, see Idem, *The Johannine Son of Man* (Biblioteca di Scienze Religiose 14; Rome: LAS, 1978) pp. 23-41.
10 Translation from M. Staniforth, *Early Christian Writings. The Apostolic Fathers* (Penguin Classics; Harmondsworth: Penguin Books, 1968) p. 80. Here I am not taking a position on the long debate over Ignatius' familiarity with the Fourth Gospel. For a survey of the discussion, see C. K. Barrett, *The Gospel According to St John* (London: SPCK, 1978) pp. 63-64. It is widely recognised that Ignatius has a 'word' theology, but it may not be dependent upon the Fourth Gospel.

1. It is important to remember that the Gospel must be read from beginning to end. The 'story' of the Gospel flows from episode to episode.[11] Within this narrative structure, the woman, the mother of Jesus is the *first* person to come to faith. In this we can see that John continues a traditional motif concerning the faith of the mother of Jesus which we met for the first time in the Gospel of Matthew (1:16), and which dominated our analysis of the Lucan material. Also in the Fourth Gospel, Mary is the first of all believers.

2. Although I have attempted to show the parallel between 2:1-11 and 4:46-54, as both the mother of Jesus and the royal official show their radical openness to the 'word' of Jesus, it is now important to notice that they do this in different ways. While the royal official 'believed the word that Jesus spoke to him' (4:50), the mother of Jesus actively communicates her faith and trust in his word by telling the servants: 'Do whatever he tells you' (2:5). There is an important link between these words of Mary, initiating 'the hour' of her son, the process which will produce a new people of God (especially in 19:25-27), and the words of the assembled people of Israel at the foot of Mt. Sinai, receiving the Law from the hands of Moses. On three occasions the assembled Israelites, committing themselves as a people of God, cry out: 'All that the Lord has spoken we will do' (Exod 19:8; 24:3, 7). These words from a crucial moment in the history of God's people are now repeated as the mother of Jesus communicates her faith in the word of her son.

Already in 2:1-11, the mother of Jesus plays an active role in initiating a process which will lead to the disciples seeing the glory of God and believing in Jesus (2:11). Many themes intertwine here, with the mother of Jesus involved in all of them: the revelation of the glory of God in Jesus, the beginning of 'the hour of Jesus', the promise of the messianic fulness at some future time, at the completion of 'the hour' (see 2:4 and 19:27). Through it all, a new way to God is founded, directed by the mother of Jesus which repeats what the older covenanted people had promised: to do whatever he says. The new people will no longer be founded on the gift of the Law, but on the

[11] On this, see the important work of J. Navone – T. Cooper, *Tellers of the Word* (New York: Le Jacq Publishing, 1981) pp. 66-92.

gift of the Word of Jesus Christ (see 1:17). His mother points the way.[12]

3. What is further unique to the Fourth Gospel is the association of the woman, the mother of Jesus, with 'the hour'. At Cana she is told: 'My hour has not yet come'. This is the first reference to a theme which will grow as the Gospel unfolds.[13] It will be the moment of Jesus' violent end (see 7:4, 30; 8:20; 12:27) but – strangely – also the moment of his glorification (see 12:33; 13:31), through which he will return to his Father (13:1, 32; 17:5). 'The hour' is a given event in the human, historical experience of Jesus of Nazareth planned by the Father for the Son. But at Cana the mother, the woman, has been inevitably drawn into its horror . . . and its power. The mother stands at the very beginnings of Jesus' 'hour' as woman and mother (see 2:1, 2, 4, 5). It is her intervention which initiates a miracle showing all the signs of being the messianic moment: the super-abundance of the best of all wines (vv. 6-10. See Gen 9:20; 49:16-22; Amos 9:13; Hos 2:24; Joel 4:18; 29:17; Jer 31:5) at a wedding feast (see Is 25:6-8; Mt 22:1-14; 25:1-13; Rev 19:7-9).[14] However, 'the hour' of the Messiah has 'not yet come'. When it does come (see 12:23; 13:1; 17:1; 19:17-37), the woman, the mother of Jesus, will again be there (19:25-27).

The hour of the woman ... and the disciples

As I have just hinted, there is a close relationship between the themes of 'the woman', the mother of Jesus and 'the hour' in the

---

[12] For a full study of the background and significance of 2:5b, see A. M. Serra, *Contributi dell'antica letteratura giudaica per l'esegesi di Giovanni 2:1-12 e 19:25-27* (Scripta Pontificiae Facultatis Theologicae 'Marianum' 31; Rome: Herder, 1977) pp. 139-181.

[13] For a study of the Johannine theme of 'the hour of Jesus', see G. Ferraro, *L'ora' di Cristo nel Quarto Vangelo* (Aloisiana 10; Roma: Herder, 1974). For a briefer survey, see F. J. Moloney, *The Word Became Flesh*, pp. 101-111.

[14] The interpretation of the miracle story itself in 2:1-11 is widely discussed, both in terms of its tradition history and its background. For an interpretation of the final Johannine redaction along the lines which I have suggested here, see H. van den Bussche, *Jean: Commentaire de l'Évangile Spirituel* (Paris: Desclée de Brouwer, 1967) pp. 146-150; B. Lindars, *The Gospel of John* (New Century Bible; London: Oliphants, 1972) p. 125; R. Schnackenburg, *The Gospel According to St John* (London/New York: Burns & Oates/Crossroad, 1968-1982) Vol. 1, pp. 329-331; R. E. Brown et alii (eds.), *Mary in the New Testament*, pp. 186-194. For an excellent discussion, see G. Zevini, *Vangelo secondo Giovanni* (Commenti Spirituali del Nuovo Testamento; Rome: Citta Nuova, 1984-1987) Vol. 1, pp. 102-115. For a survey, with full bibliographical indications, see again A. Serra, Art. 'Bibbia', in S. De Fiores – S. Meo (eds.), *Nuovo Dizionario di Mariologia*, pp. 274-284.

first miracle at Cana (2:1-11) and the reappearance of the same themes in the Johannine crucifixion scene (19:25-27). The new element at the Cross, however, is the active presence of the Beloved Disciple. Already at Cana, disciples came to faith as they saw the 'glory' of Jesus revealed in the miracle (2:11), but they have played no active part in the events of the miracle itself. They are merely 'there' (see 2:2). As the Johannine narrative of the life and death of Jesus comes to an end, however, the disciple is central to the final appearance of Jesus with his mother in the Fourth Gospel (see 19:25-27).

Interestingly, the scene at the Cross in the Fourth Gospel is not the first time that Jesus has addressed his disciples through the use of a woman, a mother. At the heart of John 16:4-33, which deals with the hour of Jesus' departure and the need to change sorrow into joy, one finds a brief but powerful use of a woman in the pains of childbirth.[15] Jesus uses this image of the movement from suffering to joy to instruct his disciples on the need to be open and receptive to the gift of God, in an attitude of prayerful asking:

> When a *woman* is in travail she has sorrow, because her *hour* has come; but *when she is delivered of the child*, she no longer remembers the anguish, for joy that a child is born to the world. So you have sorrow now, but I will see you again and your hearts will rejoice, and no one will take your joy from you. In that day you will ask nothing of me. Truly, truly I say to you, if you ask anything of the Father, he will give it to you in my name. Hitherto you have asked nothing in my name; ask, and you will receive, that your joy may be full (16:21-24).[16]

The whole section of 16:4-33 can be understood as the development and intertwining of three basic issues:

1. In vv. 4-20 Jesus instructs his disciples that he must depart from them. His departure will necessarily create pain among the disciples as they feel his loss: 'Truly, truly I say to you, you

---

[15] For a detailed discussion of this section of the Last Discourse, see Y. Simoens', *La gloire d'aimer*, pp. 151-173. On 16:21-24, see pp. 163-167. My suggestions arise from Simoens analysis, but carry them further in relating them to 2:1-11 and 19:25-27.

[16] I have accentuated the three features in 16:21 which link this passage to the traditional Johannine Marian passages (2:1-11 and 19:25-27): woman, hour and – although the term 'mother' is not found – the use of image of childbirth, uniquely and intimately associated with a mother.

will weep and lament, but the world will rejoice; you will be sorrowful' (v. 20).

2. However, in vv. 21-24 (at the centre of the whole passage) these same disciples are instructed that such sorrow can and must be turned into joy. Jesus tells his disciples how this will take place, basing himself upon the image of the woman in child-birth, whose pain turns into joy.

3. The final part of the instruction (vv. 25-33) returns to the theme of pain, suffering and trial. However now, after the indications of vv. 21-24, a new note of trust and peace in the midst of trials is powerfully present: 'In the world you have tribulation, but be of good cheer, I have overcome the world' (16:33).

The argument of vv. 21-24 depends entirely on Jesus' play upon a change of heart which takes place according to a time scheme: *now* and *afterwards*. In the case of 'the woman', she experiences sorrow *now*, because her 'hour' has come. Her anguish turns to joy *afterwards* because a child is born into the world (v. 21). 'The woman' provides Jesus with the model for his disciples. *Now* they have sorrow, but *afterwards* they will rejoice because Jesus will come to them (v. 22a). They will then be in a situation of joy which no one can take from them (vv. 22b-23a).

However, they still have a lot to learn concerning the way in which Jesus will come to them. Up to now they have asked for nothing in the name of Jesus, but if they will ask, then *after* such asking they will have anything that they seek from the Father (vv. 23b-24a). This is the new presence of Jesus to his community of disciples, a presence which can only be had through the painful experience of the loss of Jesus, and the felt need to turn to the Father in prayer. This change of situation, where it is the Father who determines both the destiny of Jesus and the future joy of the disciples is succinctly and accurately summed up in Jesus' prayer to his Father: 'But now I am coming to thee; and these things I speak in the world, that they may have my joy fulfilled in them-selves' (17:13).[17] John 16:21-24 concludes with an imperative,

---

[17] It appears to me that the theme of 'the hour' is also crucial for a correct understanding of John 17:1-26. Thus, as Mary was drawn into the hour in 2:1-11, and as 'the woman' is used to indicate the passage from suffering to joy through the hour in 16:21, Jesus' prayer to his Father (17:1-26) asks that the disciples also be caught up into that same hour. On this, see F. J. Moloney, 'John 17: The Prayer of Jesus' Hour', *The Clergy Review* 67 (1982) 79-83.

promising the disciples that joy which belongs to 'the woman': 'Ask, and you will receive, that your joy may be full' (v. 24b).

Starting from the remarkable presence of the terms 'the woman' and 'the hour', within the profoundly maternal context of giving birth, is it possible that we have here the bridge between the mother of Jesus' request setting 'the hour' of Jesus in motion, and thus associating herself with it, and the final acting out of that association – along with the Beloved Disciple – in 19:25-27? It is at this stage of the developing argument of the Johannine Gospel that 'the woman' associated with 'the hour' is presented to the disciples.[18]

It has been widely recognised that the Johannine use of the term 'the woman' has symbolic power. It means more than just the historical Mary. At this stage of the developing understanding of the person and role of Mary in the history of salvation, links are being made from Mary, the mother of Jesus, back to the figure of Eve, and from there to 'the woman' doing battle with the serpent in Gen 3:15.[19]

This sort of reflection, which was probably widely spread in the latter part of the first century (see especially Rev 12:1-6), forms part of the background for the Johannine use of the term 'woman'. A further major part of his background, however, which we must not be lose sight of in the richness of the symbol from Genesis 3:15, is the fact that the person in question was 'a woman'!

Nevertheless, it may have been at the crossroad between the profoundly symbolic level and the early Church's reflections on the actual experience of the mother of Jesus that 16:21-24 links the two Johannine explicitly Marian scenes. What is described in the experience of 'the woman' in v. 21 was a process initiated in

---

[18] It is my firm belief that no matter what may have been the long and complicated history of the traditions behind the Fourth Gospel, the Gospel as we now have it is a narrative marked by a unified literary and theological design. However brilliant some of his insights into the Gospel may sometimes be, Bultmann's claim that the final form of the Gospel is an accidental gathering of disorganised and misplaced traditions cannot be sustained. See, R. Bultmann, *The Gospel of John. A Commentary* (Oxford: Basil Blackwell, 1971) passim. For my view of the Fourth Gospel's literary and theological unity, see F. J. Moloney, *The Living Voice of the Gospel*, pp. 161-201. See also R. Culpepper, *Anatomy of the Fourth Gospel. A Study in Literary Design* (Foundation and Facets; Philadelphia: Fortress Press, 1983).

[19] See the excellent synthesis, with further references to both Patristic and further secondary literature in R. E. Brown, *The Gospel According to John* (The Anchor Bible 29-29a; New York: Doubleday, 1966-1970) Vol. 1, pp. 107-109.

2:1-11, in the mother of Jesus' association with 'the hour'. There is the anguish of a birth which she must experience, initiated but 'not yet' at Cana. She must hand her Son back to the Father (see 13:1; 17:5), and bear further fruit, through the pain of this 'hour', in being one with and mother of the disciple in the Church born at the Cross (19:25-27). Within the context of Jesus' final discourse to his disciples (16:21-24), the Johannine Jesus presents the passage of 'the woman', a mother giving birth through her 'hour', from anguish to joy (v. 21). He thus indicates the path which the disciples themselves must tread if they wish to have the fulness of joy (vv. 22-24).

In his analysis of the background and meaning of the Johannine use of the mother of Jesus as 'the woman', Raymond Brown has described this passage and its relationship to the Johannine Marian material aptly when he wrote:

> John thinks of Mary against the background of Gen 3: she is the mother of the Messiah; her role is in the struggle against the satanic serpent, and that struggle comes to its climax in Jesus' hour. Then she will appear at the foot of the cross to be entrusted with offspring whom she must protect in the continuing struggle between Satan and the followers of the Messiah.[20]

Her association with the hour of Jesus, initiated in 2:4, will come to its fruitful climax in 19:27: 'From that hour, he took her into his own home'. Her personal anguish which leads to joy, and the association of that anguish leading to joy with the life of the disciple is indicated in 16:21-24. It is finally and dramatically spelt out in 19:25-27.

Woman, mother and disciple at the hour of the Cross

It is widely recognised that the Johannine passion account is a careful rewriting of the traditional passion story, marked by a lessening of the descriptions of insult and agony, and a

---

[20] *Ibid.*, p. 109. Brown, *ibid.*, Vol 2, pp. 731-732 makes reference to this possibility in his comment on 16:21, but does not commit himself to the position. He has since communicated to me that he regards a connection between 16:21 and the other Johannine Marian material as 'very possible'. This does not, of course, mean that he would agree with my case nor the arguments of Feuillet. See the contributions of A. Feuillet mentioned above in note 3.

heightening of the theme of the kingship of Jesus which is already to be found in the Gospel of Mark.[21]

As is customary in the Fourth Gospel, the very structure of the passion narrative, in five major scenes, is a first indication of the sophistication of the narrative. It is structured concentrically, around a central and major narrative (the trial before Pilate), in the following way:

A. Gethsemane: Jesus in a Garden, encounters his enemies (18:1-11).

B. The Jewish trial: The witnessing to the truth on the part of Jesus, matched by the failure of Peter: Overall theme: *The Church* (18:12-27).

C. THE TRIAL BEFORE PILATE: JESUS IS BOTH PRO-CLAIMED AND CROWNED AS *KING* (18:28 – 19:16).

B1. The Crucifixion: Jesus, reigning as King from his Cross, founds the Church, and pours down his Spirit upon it: Overall theme: *The Church* (19:17-37).

A1. The Burial: Jesus in a Garden with his friends (19:38-42).

There is a balance between the two garden scenes. Jesus first encounters the powers of darkness, coming to arrest him carrying swords and lanterns (18:3). At the end of the passion story (19:38-42) he is finally laid to rest with the splendour fit only for a king by two newly-found friends who have come out from the darkness of fear to publicly ask for the honour of burying Jesus (Nicodemus [see 3:1] and Joseph of Arimathea [19:38-39]). A similar balance is found between the two scenes devoted to the theme of the Church, one highlighting its fragility in the failure of Peter (18:15-18,

---

[21] On the Johannine passion account, as well as the commentaries, see (among many) R. E. Brown, 'The Passion According to John: Chapters 18-19', *Worship* 49 (1975) 126-134; I. de la Potterie, 'La passion selon S. Jean', *Assemblées du Seigneur* 21 (1969) 21-34; J. C. Fenton, *The Passion According to John* (London, SPCK, 1961); E. Haenchen, 'History and Interpretation in the Johannine Passion Narrative', *Interpretation* 24 (1970) 198-219; A. E. Harvey, *Jesus on Trial. A Study in the Fourth Gospel* (London: SPCK, 1976); G. C. Nicholson, *Death as Departure. The Johannine Descent-Ascent Scheme* (SBL Dissertation Series 63; Chico: Scholars Press, 1983); D. M. Stanley, 'The Passion According to John', *Worship* 33 (1958-59) 213-230; W. A. Meeks, *The Prophet-King. Moses Traditions and the Johannine Christology* (Supplements to Novum Testamentum 14; Leiden: E. J. Brill, 1967) pp. 61-81. On the theme of Jesus as King in Mark's passion account, see D. Senior, *The Passion of Jesus in the Gospel of Mark* (The Passion Series 2; Wilmington: Michael Glazier, 1984) pp. 105-114; F. J. Matera, *The Kingship of Jesus. Composition and Theology in Mark 15* (SBL Dissertation Series 66; Chico: Scholars Press, 1982).

25-27),[22] the other featuring the founding of the Church by the crucified King (19:17-37).

In the central scene, the trial before Pilate, Jesus is proclaimed as a king (18:35-37, 39; 19:3, 7, 14); he is crowned and clothed as a king (19:1-3), and he acts as a king (18:33-38; 19:5, 8-11, 13).[23] But such proclamations, coronations and actions are continually and explicitly refused (18:38, 40; 19:3, 6, 12, 15 [as a climax: 'We have no king but Caesar!']).

It is within this overall context that our final Marian scene in the Fourth Gospel is found (19:25-27). Thus far I have only spoken of the crucifixion scene as Jesus' kingly action in both founding and pouring down his Spirit upon the Church. A little more detailed analysis will show that the account of the mother of Jesus and the Beloved Disciple at the foot of the cross (19:25-27) is the central scene in a series of five separate scenes, all of which are in some way concerned with the Johannine message of the crucified Jesus and the foundation of the Church.

Once Jesus is crucified (19:17-18), the kingship of Jesus is universally proclaimed in Latin, Greek and Hebrew through the title on the Cross: 'Jesus of Nazareth, the King of the Jews' (v. 19). Although this proclamation is refused (v. 21) it remains because it is true (v. 22). The scene which follows, dealing with the seamless garment (vv. 23-25a), is a sign that the intimate possession of Jesus (soon to be seen as the Church) will not be torn apart, not even in the

---

[22] This 'ecclesial' interpretation of the denials of Peter was recognised by the Johannine community itself. It stands behind the section of John 21, added to the Gospel by the community after the original Gospel had been written, which deals explicitly with the role of Peter. As he had denied Jesus three times, his role as the pastor of the flock of Jesus depends upon his threefold profession of love (see 21:15-19).

[23] On the trial before Pilate, as well as the commentaries and the studies mentioned above in note 21, see the more detailed suggestions of J. Blank, 'Die Verhandlung vor Pilatus: Joh 18:28-19:16 im Lichte der johanneischen Theologie', *Biblische Zeitschrift* 3 (1959) 60-81; I. de la Potterie, 'Jésus roi et juge d'après Jn. 19:13 *"Ekathisen epi bēmatos"* ', *Biblica* 41 (1960) 317-347; E. Haenchen, 'Jesus vor Pilatus (Joh 18:28-19:16). Zur Methode der Auslegung', in *Gott und Mensch. Gesammelte Aufsätze* (Tübingen: J. C. B. Mohr [Paul Siebeck], 1965) pp. 144-156; F. Hahn, 'Der Prozess Jesu nach dem Johannesevangelium. Eine redaktionsgeschichtliche Untersuchung', *Evangelisch-katholisches Kommentar zum Neuen Testament Vorbereitung* 2 (Köln: Benzinger, 1970) pp. 23-76; D. Mollat, 'Jésus devant Pilate (Jean 18:28-19:16)', *Bible et Vie Chrétienne* 39 (1961) 23-31; F. J. Moloney, *The Johannine Son of Man* pp. 202-207.

hands of the enemies.[24] At the centre of the Johannine Cross account, the third of five more detailed scenes, stands the gift of mother to son and son to mother. The scene which immediately follows is the death of Jesus (vv. 28-30) where the dying Jesus can exclaim that he has brought to perfection all that he was sent to do (see, in this connection, 4:34 and 17:4), bow his head and 'pour down' the Spirit.[25] Finally, the Evangelist, to assure his Church at the end of the first century of the presence of the absent crucified one, speaks passionately and eloquently of the blood and water flowing from his side (vv. 31-37). It is in their own baptised and eucharistic lives that 'they shall look upon him whom they have pierced' (v. 37).[26]

Given the powerfully ecclesiological message of the whole of the Johannine story of the Cross, it stands to reason that the scene at the very centre of the narrative will also be primarily ecclesiological. But while such is indeed the case, it is a Church where a 'mother' and a 'disciple' play a crucial role. Jesus is 'lifted up' on the Cross (see 3:14; 8:28; 12:32), proclaimed as King (19:19). The reader now knows, from the account of the soldiers' handling of his inner garment, that the Church will never be divided. He now founds his 'new family'. However, unlike Mark (see Mk 3:31-35) it is not only disciples who form this family. Crucial to its beginnings is his mother (19:25-27). The deliberate care which the Fourth Evangelist has taken to place the mother and the disciple at the

---

[24] The scene has been rightly interpreted in this way by the Fathers of the Church. See, M. Aubineau, 'La tunique sans couture du Christ. Exéèse patristique de Jean 19:13-24', in P. Granfield – J. A. Jungmann (eds.) *Kyriakon. Festschrift Johannes Quasten* (Münster: Aschendorff, 1970) Vol. I, pp. 100-127.

[25] Although most commentators allude to this possibility, most refuse to accept it, as they see the gift of the Spirit taking place in the upper room in 20:22. It appears to me that this is too narrow. The whole of the Gospel points towards the cross as the moment of the 'lifting up' of Jesus (see 3:14; 8:28; 12:32), an essential part of his glorification (see 11:4; 12:23; 13:31-32). Already in 7:37-39 – where the plot to kill Jesus thickens (see 7:1, 5-6, 19, 25, 30 ['the hour'], 44, 47-49) – there has been a close link drawn between the death of Jesus, the glorification of Jesus and the gift of the Spirit, associated with living water flowing from his side. This *must* be a reference to 19:30 (see the immediately following vv. 34-35). It is also important to notice that whatever our translations might say, the Greek text does not say that 'he bowed his head and *gave up his spirit'* [RSV]. It says that 'he gave *down the* spirit' (*paredôken to pneuma*).

[26] On this, see E. Malatesta, 'Blood and Water from the Pierced Side of Christ', in P.-R. Tragan (ed.), *Segni e Sacramenti nel Vangelo di Giovanni* (Studia Anselmiana 66, Sacramentum 3; Rome: Editrice Anselmiana, 1977) pp. 164-181; F. J. Moloney, 'When is John Talking about Sacraments?', *Australian Biblical Review* 30 (1982) 10-33.

Cross in this climactic moment for his story and his theology of Jesus must be given its full value.

The two figures at the foot of the Cross have played an important role in the Gospel itself. We have already seen that the mother of Jesus, 'the woman', has been associated with the hour of Jesus from the very beginnings of his public ministry (2:1-11) and that 'the woman' was used by Jesus, in his final discourse, to show how one should pass from sadness to joy through the experience of 'the hour' (16:21). Now that the hour has come (see 12:23; 13:1; 17:1), the mother of Jesus, 'the woman', reappears. However, we also learnt from our analysis of 2:1-11 that the mother of Jesus led the way as the first among all believers. She was the first to come to faith, prepared to entrust herself completely to the word of Jesus: 'Do whatever he tells you' (2:5). This action, in turn, led to the initial faith of the first disciples (see 2:11).

The Beloved Disciple is the unnamed disciple who has leant upon the breast of Jesus at the supper in the upper room (13:21-26). It is this same disciple who will come to faith at the empty tomb, after outrunning the more sluggish Peter.[27] We are dealing with Johannine models of faith and love, 'the woman' who is the 'mother of Jesus', and the 'disciple whom Jesus loved'.

A careful reading of the passage shows that the Fourth Evangelist has the crucified King address his mother and the Beloved Disciple in a way which explicitly calls upon a pattern of revelation. This pattern comes to him from the biblical tradition.[28] Jesus saw his mother and the disciple, he *said* to his mother: '*Behold!*', and he said to the disciple '*Behold!*'. This pattern is used by the prophets when they speak authoritatively in the name of Yahweh (see, for example, Is 49:18; 60:4; Bar 4:36-37; 5:5; Ezek 1:4 − 3:11; 37:7-14; Dan 2:31-45). In the prophets and in this scene at the Cross in the Fourth Gospel the same elements appear: sight, address, a command, 'Behold', leading to a revelation of the ways and will

---

[27] The discussion of the identity and the role of the Beloved Disciple in the Fourth Gospel is never-ending. For my own reflections, see F. J. Moloney, *The Word Became Flesh*, pp. 14-18. See also ibid., 'John 20: A Journey Completed', *Australasian Catholic Record* 59 (1982) 417-432. This article should now be read in the light of the further suggestions of B. J. Byrne, 'The Faith of the Beloved Disciple and the Community in John 20', *Journal for the Study of the New Testament* 23 (1985) 83-97.

[28] On this, see M. de Goedt, 'Un schème de révélation dans le Quatrième Evangile', *New Testament Studies* 8 (1961-62) 142-150.

of God. For the Fourth Evangelist, the crucified Son of God is revealing the will and the ways of God by means of this formula as he solemnly establishes a new relationship between his mother and his disciple.

The overall context of the Gospel and of the Johannine passion account, the characters in the scene at the Cross (Jesus, his mother and the beloved disciple) and the deliberate use of a formula of revelation all blend to show that 'the hour' is fulfilled and the Church is founded at this moment. The first of all believers, the woman who associated herself with the hour of Jesus from the first moments of his public life, cost her what it may, is joined to the disciple whom Jesus loved. The beloved disciple is also a great believer: he is the first of all disciples to come to faith in the risen Lord (20:8). The mother is given to the disciple, and thus the Church is born.

There is still more to the scene. The mother of Jesus and the disciple play a role at the Cross which makes them the representative symbols of all the children of God, gathered together by the Son of Man 'lifted up' from the earth (see 3:13-14; 8:28; 12:32-33; 11:51-52). Throughout the latter part of the Gospel there has been a growing theme which reaches its climax with the mother and the disciple at the Cross: the theme of the 'gathering' of all the dispersed ones around the crucified but exalted Jesus.[29] The use of the mother and the disciple at the foot of the Cross comes as the conclusion to a theme which indicates that they represent much more than two people who were dear to Jesus.[30]

In the discourse on the Good Shepherd where the Cross looms large, Jesus announces:

And I have other sheep, that are not of this fold; I must bring them also, and they will heed my voice. So there shall be one flock, one shepherd (10:16).

---

[29] This theme has been noticed and sensitively researched by A. M. Serra, *Contributi dell'antica letteratura giudaica*, pp. 303-429. What follows is slightly different. Serra uses John 6:44-46; 10:16; 11:52; 12:32 and 17:21. While the theme is certainly there, I will introduce some further texts which centre the 'gathering' theme more firmly on the crucifixion.

[30] Some commentators miss the theological importance of this aspect of 19:25-27 completely. A good example (among several) is E. Haenchen, *John* (Hermeneia; Philadelphia: Fortress Press, 1984) Vol. 2, p. 200: 'Jesus cares for those close to him, and he is not foresaken (sic.) by them, even in death'.

He immediately indicates how the gathering and the formation of the one flock will take place: by laying down his life for his sheep (vv. 17-18).

After Caiaphas has announced that Jesus must die for the nation, the Evangelist adds a further explanation: 'And not for the nation only, but to gather into one the children of God who are scattered abroad' (11:52). The death of Jesus will lead to a gathering of the scattered children of God. With Jesus' anointing and entry into Jerusalem the passion of Jesus begins . . . but so does the 'gathering'. Afraid of Jesus' attraction, the chief priests plan to slay both Lazarus and Jesus, because on account of the former's resurrection 'many of the Jews were going away and believing in Jesus' (12:11). The concluding remark from the Pharisees, after Jesus' entry into the city makes it clear that it is no longer only a question of 'many of the Jews': 'You see that you can do nothing; look, the *world* has gone after him' (12:19). As if to prove them correct, the very next scene in the Johannine narrative is the arrival of the Greeks saying: 'We wish to see Jesus' (12:21). The Jews and the whole world seek and believe in Jesus, because 'the hour' has come.

There has been more than a hint through all of these passages which speak of the 'gathering' that the Cross is the place where it will take place. After the arrival of the Greeks, it becomes quite explicit that such is the case. On being told that the Greeks are seeking him, Jesus responds:

The hour has come for the Son of man to be glorified. Truly, truly I say to you, unless a grain of wheat falls into the earth and dies, it *remains alone*; but if it dies, it bears much fruit (12:23-24).

The final and definitive statement from Jesus, linking the 'gathering' with the Cross comes towards the end of this same discourse, which concludes the public life of Jesus in the Fourth Gospel:

Now is the judgment of this world, now shall the ruler of this world be cast out; and I, when I am lifted up from the earth, *will draw all men to myself*. He said this to show by what death he was to die (12:31-33).

These two passages from chapter 12 state and re-state the same theme: the grain must fall and die, or else it will remain alone; Jesus will be 'lifted up' in death, and thus draw women and men from all ages and places to himself. He will not 'remain alone'.[31]

In his death on the Cross this promise is 'perfected', as Jesus brings to a consummate conclusion the task which the Father had given him to do (see 4:34; 17:4). He has 'gathered' the Church at his feet in the persons of his mother and his disciple and he pours the Spirit on the newly founded family (19:30).[32] The mother and the disciple are used to 'represent' the gathering which takes place – down through the ages – at the Cross of Jesus (see, in this sense, 19:37). Little wonder that the Evangelist concludes the scene at the Cross with his final use of a major theological term which first appeared at the instigation of the mother of Jesus in 2:1-11: 'And from *that hour* the disciple took her to his own home'.

My analysis of 19:25-27 has highlighted the ecclesiological significance of this central passage in the Johannine crucifixion story. I have also shown, however, that the narrative is carried by three characters who are of great importance to the Johannine point of view: Jesus (obviously!), the mother of Jesus and the Beloved Disciple. If the message on the Church were the only theological issue which John wished to communicate through 19:25-27, then one can understand that 'the disciple' must play a crucial role, as disciples are crucial to the founding resurrection narratives in the synoptic tradition.[33] But why does 'the mother of Jesus' play such

---

[31] J. E. Morgan-Wynne, 'The Cross and the Revelation of Jesus as *ego eimi* in the Fourth Gospel', in E. A. Livingstone (ed.), *Studia Biblica II. Papers on the Gospels*, pp. 219-226 introduces 16:32 to a discussion of Jesus' being 'lifted up', claiming that even the Fourth Evangelist presents Jesus as abandoned and alone on the Cross. A more wide-reaching use of texts related to the theme of the Cross shows that the opposite is the case.

[32] It is important to notice that there is a tight causal link between 19:25-27 and the scene which follows (vv. 28-30) which concentrates on Jesus' having brought to perfection the task which he was given by his Father. This link is created by the Johannine expression *meta touto* ('after this') in v. 28a. It is only *because* he has given his mother to the disciple, and the disciple to his mother – that he has in fact initiated the 'gathering' at the Cross – that he can now claim to have perfectly fulfilled the task which the Father gave him. On this, see A. Serra, Art. 'Bibbia', in S. De Fiores – S. Meo, *Nuovo Dizionario di Mariologia*, p. 285

[33] Many of the themes which are found in the resurrection narratives in the synoptic tradition are found in the death of Jesus in the Fourth Gospel. This is certainly the case with the Johannine theology of the Church. R. E. Brown, *John*, Vol. 2, p. 912 puts it well:'The principal episodes of the crucifixion are concerned with the gifts that the enthroned king gives to those who accept his kingdom. . . . The Johannine crucifixion scene is, in a certain way, less concerned with the fate of Jesus than with the significance of that fate for his followers'.

a prominent role? She does not appear at either the cross or the empty tomb in the synoptic tradition. Only in the Fourth Gospel is 'the woman, the mother' at the Cross. In fact, the term 'mother' appears no less than five times in these three short verses.[34] The mother of Jesus does not simply stand at the Cross. She is not merely a static observer, weeping at the death of her son, as so much of our iconography seems to portray. There is a *relationship* established at the Cross, a relationship which has its origins in that which existed between a mother and a son (2:1-11; 19:25), and its end in the disciple's taking her 'to his own home' (v. 27). The relationship established between these two foundational figures in the community of Jesus which is born at the cross is that of mother-son and son-mother. The mother of Jesus has become the mother of the disciple.

The relationship which has just been established is, as we have seen, the result of a specific command of Jesus, made in the name of God through a revelation formula. The final indication of the nature and the purpose of this relationship is all too briefly described in v. 27b: 'And from (or 'because of'?) that hour the disciple took her to his own home'. The disciple, we are told, took her *eis ta idia* as a chronological, and probably causal, consequence of 'that hour'.[35] We are forced to translate the Greek expression *eis ta idia*

---

[34] Many commentators are able to see the ecclesial significance of the scene, but baulk at its possible mariological interpretation. See, for example, E. C. Hoskyns – F. N. Davey (ed.), *The Fourth Gospel* (London: Faber & Faber, 1947) p. 530; C. K. Barrett, *The Gospel According to St John* (London: SPCK, 1978) pp. 547-548; F. F. Bruce, *The Gospel of John* (Basingstoke: Pickering Paperbacks, 1983) pp. 371-372. R. Bultmann, *The Gospel of John*, p. 673 sees the scene as a symbolic unification of Jewish Christianity (the mother) and Gentile Christianity (the disciple). Bultmann has rightly seen the symbolic significance of the two figures, and also that the scene at the Cross fulfills the promise of the 'gathering' of the children of God scattered abroad (see 11:52). However, his precise identification of the 'children' represented has no basis in the text. See C. H. Dodd, *The Interpretation of the Fourth Gospel* (Cambridge: University Press, 1953) p. 428 who, against Bultmann, claims that any attempt to give the passage a symbolic meaning is 'singularly unconvincing'. Similarly E. Haenchen, *John 2*, p. 193 has more recently commented: 'There is nothing in the story that points to such a symbolic meaning for these figures'. While not agreeing with Bultmann's identifications, the symbol of the mother of Jesus and the Beloved Disciple appears very obvious to me, and very much a part of the Gospel's 'story'.

[35] The emphatic final use of 'the hour' at the very beginning of the sentence accompanied by the demonstrative adjective 'that' in the expression *ap'ekeinês tês hôras* indicates its importance for the interpretation of the passage. The preposition *apo* followed by the genitive case (as here) can mean 'from', in the sense of separation from, or it can have a causal sense: 'because of, for'. See, F. Blass – A. Debrunner – R. W. Funk, *A Greek Grammar of the New Testament and Other Early Christian Literature* (Chicago: The

as 'into his own home', but the absolute use of *ta idia* (neuter plural) is found in only one other place in the Gospel: 'He came unto his own (*ta idia*), but his very own people did not receive him' (1:11). The mother is now part of a new people who live by faith and love – the Church of Jesus Christ. There is now a place and a people which can be called *ta idia*, and where Jesus will be received. The mother of Jesus, 'the woman' who now becomes a 'mother' in this new situation will lead the way in that process (see 16:21). Her relationship to the Church is not only as another disciple. She is not 'sister' to the disciple, she is not just another member of *ta idia*, this new place and people. She is 'Mother'.

The Fourth Evangelist has brought the New Testament reflection on the person and place of Mary in God's story among us to a conclusion.[36] He has continued the developments which began with the simple facts of Jesus' being born of a woman, his mother Mary. Matthew and Luke have shown us that the early Church continued to interpret the significance of this woman and mother still further. John has embraced their conclusions, but carried them further. It is fascinating that the earliest terms used to speak of Mary: 'woman' and 'mother' reappear at the end of the New Testament's development – but now 'the woman' embodies the hopes of all humankind, and she is the Mother of the Church.

University of Chicago Press, 1961) paras. 209-210. I would suggest that perhaps *both* meanings are involved in 19:27.

[36] Some readers may be surprised that I have not used 'the woman clothed with the sun' from Rev 12:1 in this reflection. I regard this passage, along with the further use of 'woman' imagery in chs. 17 and 21, as most important witnesses to the early Church's reflection on 'the woman'. In this way, they are indeed related to the Marian material. See, on this, F. J. Moloney, *Woman: First among the Faithful*, pp. 65-73. However, like John 16:21 which has its literary context between two explicitly Marian passages, this famous 'woman' text must also be interpreted within the message of 'the woman' in Revelation. Unlike the Fourth Gospel, Mary herself does not appear in that document. I am aware that the Church has often used Rev 12 with a Marian interpretation, and it is often read in the Roman Liturgy for Marian celebrations. See *Redemptoris Mater* 47 which speaks of the relationship between Mary and Rev 12:1 as an 'ecclesial identification'. Again, for an excellent survey, see A. Serra, Art. 'Bibbia', in S. De Fiores – S. Meo (eds.), *Nuovo Dizionario di Mariologia*, pp. 292-301.

Chapter 6
Conclusion

It is well known that the Fathers of the Second Vatican Council debated the issue of its Marian statement at great length, and that the final decision to place it within the context of *Lumen Gentium*, the document on the Church, was only narrowly won in the closing stages of the debate. While there was strong support for a statement of Mary's role within the Church, many other Fathers felt that this did not say enough concerning her relationship to Christ, or the roots of the Marian mystery within the Trinity itself.[1]

The Council's final decision to place Mary firmly within the pilgrim Church as the one 'who occupies a place in the Church which is the highest after Christ and also closest to us' (*Lumen Gentium* 54) has flowed on into post-conciliar Marian studies. Most contemporary biblical studies of Mary tend to focus their attention on the role of Mary as the perfect disciple.[2] From the New Testament material which we have analysed, it should be clear that this is indeed a valid approach with a solid basis in the texts themselves. However, it appears to me that the inspired writings of the

---

[1]   For a study of the history of the development of *Lumen Gentium*, see G. Philips, 'Dogmatic Constitution on the Church. History of the Constitution', in H. Vorgrimler (ed.), *Commentary on the Documents of Vatican II* (London: Burns & Oates, 1967) Vol. 1, pp. 105-137. The debate goes on. See, for example, A. Müller, 'Marias Stellung und Mitwirkung im Christusereignis', in J. Feiner – M. Löhrer (eds.), *Mysterium Salutis. Grundriss Heilsgeschichtlicher Dogmatik* (Eisiedeln: Benziger Verlag, 1969) Vol. 3/2, pp. 407-421; L. Boff, *The Maternal Face of God*, pp. 9-21; A. J. Tambasco, *What are they saying about Mary?*, pp. 38-53. For a good survey of post-conciliar Mariology, see P. Bearsley, 'The Metamorphosis of Mariology', *The Clergy Review* 49 (1984) 65-71.

[2]   See, for example, P. Bearsley, 'Mary the Perfect Disciple: a Paradigm for Mariology', *Theological Studies* 41 (1980) 461-504. Bearsley's article gives copious further references. See further, R. E. Brown, 'The Contribution of Critical Exegesis to an Understanding of Mary and Marian Doctrine', in *Biblical Exegesis & Church Doctrine* (New York: Paulist Press, 1985) pp. 86-100; B. Buby, *Mary, the Faithful Disciple* (New York: Paulist Press, 1985); H. Küng – J. Moltmann (eds.), 'Mary in the Churches', *Concilium* 168 (Edinburgh: T. & T. Clark, 1983); A. J. Tambasco, *What are they saying about Mary?*, pp. 13-37. The Marian material in my own book, *Woman: First Among the Faithful* also takes this line consistently.

New Testament should force us to widen our approach. There is a need to give more place to the very terms and concepts which dominate the literature itself: Mary, woman and mother.

From the beginnings of Christian literature she is presented as a woman and a mother (Gal 4:4; Mk 3:31-35; 6:3). As the early Church began to reflect more deeply upon the significance of her person and her place in the life of Jesus, and in God's dealings with our history, the Gospels of Matthew and Luke both continue to use exactly these same terms (see Mt 1:18, 20, 24; 2:11, 13, 14, 20, 21; Lk 1:42; 2:33, 34, 48, 51). At the end of the first century, the Fourth Evangelist uses *only* these terms. He never calls Mary by her proper name. She is only 'the woman' and 'the mother of Jesus' (see Jn 2:1-11; 16:21; 19:25-27).

As we have seen, there was a growing and deepening understanding of the significance of the expressions *woman* and *mother* as the early Church attempted to articulate the mystery of God's revelation of himself in and through Jesus of Nazareth. An understanding of the role and person of Mary, woman and the mother of Jesus, was obviously crucial to these attempts. Naturally, each Evangelist used the fundamental tradition of Mary as woman and mother in his own way, finally arriving at the Johannine presentation of 'the woman' as the perfect fulfilment of the woman doing battle with the serpent in Gen 3:15, and a 'mother' who is no longer simply the mother of Jesus, but the mother of the disciple. Even in the Fourth Gospel, however, such symbolic language was used because Mary of Nazareth was, in fact, a woman and a mother.

It would be naive, of course, for the contemporary thinker and preacher to leap immediately and uncritically from the New Testament's use of the categories of Mary as a woman and a mother into the important contemporary debates surrounding the feminine.[3] However, the issue is real and urgent. The evidence which we have

---

[3] The literature is immense. For recent attempts to develop a proper feminist 'hermeneutic' of the Bible, see E. S. Fiorenza, *In Memory of Her. A Feminist Theological Reconstruction of Christian Origins* (London: SCM Press, 1983); Idem, *Bread not Stone. The Challenge of Feminist Biblical Interpretation* (Boston: Beacon Press, 1984); M. A. Tolbert (ed.), *The Bible and Feminist Hermeneutics* (Semeia 28; Scholars Press: Chico, 1983); A.Y. Collins (ed.), *Feminist Perspectives on Biblical Scholarship* (Society of Biblical Literature Centennial Publications 10; Chico: Scholars Press, 1985). See the recent critique of some of the prevailing feminist methods by S. Heine, *Women and Early Christianity. Are the Feminist Scholars Right?* (London: SCM Press, 1987).

examined shows that the earliest Church both saw and spoke of Mary as a woman and as a mother. The world of the New Testament is not our world, but the task of translating the challenge of Mary, woman and mother, into categories which will speak to the women and men of our own times is an important one.

Although the Church has placed the maternity of Mary at the centre of its theological reflection and its cult from the days of the great debates over the *Theotokos* down to our own time,[4] are the traditional ways of presenting Mary as 'mother' still eloquent? It is one thing continually to represent Mary as the 'Mother of God', but there is another, more common, experience of being a 'mother' which she lived in full. It is this latter form of Mary's being a 'mother' which stands behind the New Testament's language and imagery. Closely associated with this is perhaps the more urgent and equally important issue of Mary as 'woman', another expression, as we have seen, dear to the authors of the New Testament. This also needs further investigation, and a more courageous evaluation.

Some directions are emerging. In a Church led by male – and very often clerical – theologians, Hans-Urs von Balthasar has pointed to Mary the woman as someone who might question our understanding of God and his ways:

> As a woman she (Mary) has her heart where it ought to be and not in the brain; and she knows that a God who thought woman up and created her can have his heart in no other place.[5]

Basil Pennington points to another rich vein directing us to look more closely to Mary for a better understanding of 'womanliness' and 'manliness' in our response to such a God when he suggests:

> There is neither male nor female in Mary, or rather both male and female are fully in her. There is an autonomy and relatedness, strength and tenderness, struggle and victory, God's power and

---

[4] The term *Theotokos* (Mother of God) was, of course, linked primarily with the great Christological debates of the 3rd-5th centuries. It is used formally, *in a conciliar statement*, for the first time at the Council of Ephesus in 431. The ongoing importance of the motherhood theme can be seen in both the title and the contents of *Redemptoris Mater* (1987). For an excellent synthesis, see Th. Koehler, Art. 'Storia della Mariologia', in S. De Fiores – S. Meo, *Nuovo Dizionario di Mariologia*, pp. 1385-1405.

[5] H.-U. von Balthasar, *Mary for Today*, p. 71. See also the few remarks along these lines in *Redemptoris Mater* 46. The Pope suggests that the issue of Mary as woman 'can be studied in greater depth elsewhere'.

human agency. There is woman. She is, like her Son and by his grace and imaging, an integrated image of God. Lest by some delusion . . . it be thought that such complete integration and imaging of Christ can only be realized in a man, God willed that there stand by Christ a perfect woman in whom this integration was fully accomplished.[6]

Both of these pointed (and polemical) affirmations present their own difficulties, but it is not the task of my concluding reflections to set out on a further study of Mary as woman through a presentation of my agreement with or dissent from such positions. They are offered as an example of the sort of questions which need to be asked. It is important that we face the questions which our New Testament study of Mary, woman and mother, pose.[7] These two scholars have seen that the figure of Mary, woman and mother, raises issues which should lead us to the further investigation of the central mysteries of Christian faith and practice: how do we understand our God, and what is the nature of our response to the love which he has revealed to us in his Son, Jesus Christ?

Wherever one takes one's stance in the contemporary theological world, the New Testament evidence makes it clear that a woman stood at the centre of the stage in God's decisive inbreak into the history of the salvation of all women and men. Her assent to the ways of God mysteriously working through her belongs to the official, public, saving history in the economy of God. These are objective truths revealed to us in the Sacred Scriptures treasured by all the Christian Churches. We would shirk our responsibilities if we did not inquire 'into the question of whether Mary as a woman who is a mother, reveals an aspect of God's life and nature; that is to say, whether womanhood and motherhood have their source in God'.[8]

---

[6] M. B. Pennington, *Mary Today*, p. 95. His whole treatment of Mary as woman is found on pp. 90-97.

[7] An early attempt to present Mary from a feminist perspective can be found in Rosemary R. Ruether, *Mary – The Feminine Face of the Church* (Philadelphia: Westminster Press, 1977). See now, Idem, *Sexism and God-Talk: Towards a Feminist Theology* (London: SCM Press, 1983) pp. 139-158. Helpful pointers towards further reflection along these lines can be found in the work of the following women: Rosemary Haughton, *The Re-Creation of Eve*, pp. 109-122; Jill Robson, 'Mary: My Sister', in Monica Furlong (ed.), *Feminine in the Church* (London: SPCK, 1984) pp. 119-138 and Ann Loades, *Searching for Lost Coins. Explorations in Christianity and Feminism* (London: SPCK, 1987) pp. 78-103.

[8] E. Doyle, 'God and the Feminine', *Clergy Review* 56 (1985) 870. The article runs from pp. 866-877, as cited by A. Loades, *Searching for Lost Coins*, p. 101. I have been unable to locate this article in *The Clergy Review*, and 1985 is Vol. 50.

Such further investigation and evaluation of Mary, as both woman and mother, should then flow into the Church's life and cult to the benefit of us all, women and men alike. There is little need for me to stress how opportune such an endeavour would be. As Catharina Halkes has written:

> It is only when the Church is bold enough to look at every aspect of the 'great mother' that full justice will be done to women and a sound Mariology will be able to have a salutary effect on women as well as men.[9]

In recognising in Mary – not only the mother of the disciple and the mother of the Church – but also as God's place of encounter with all that is most beautiful among women and men, then we will have gained access to the womanly, maternal face of God.[10]

---

[9] C. Halkes, 'Mary and Women', *Concilium* 168 (1983) 73. The article runs from pp. 66-73. Although I find myself continually at odds with the exegesis of his article, J. McKenzie, 'The Mother of Jesus in the New Testament', *Concilium* 168 (1983) 10 is correct in his intuition that men have been largely resonsible for creating 'the plaster doll of the traditional Mary'. The article runs from pp. 3-11.

[10] L. Boff, *The Maternal Face of God*, pp. 9-21 looks at the various 'organisational principles' which have been used in the study of Mary. One of these has been her maternity (see pp. 13-14). His own thought-provoking book is focused on 'the feminine as the basic mariological principle' (pp. 18-21). Here, however, the Church needs the leadership of its women, as 'there are still many male theologians who quite blandly write about Mary and femininity without taking the experiences that are expressed by women themselves into account' (Catharina Halkes, 'Mary and Women', p. 66).

Bibliography

Aubineau, M., 'La tunique sans couture du Christ. Exégèse patristique de Jean 19:13-24', in P. Granfield – J.A. Jungmann (eds.), *Kyriakon. Festschrift Johannes Quasten* (Münster: Aschendorf, 1970) Vol. I, pp. 100-127.

Baab, O.J., Article 'Virgin', in G.A. Buttrick (ed.), *The Interpreter's Dictionary of the Bible* (New York/Nashville: Abingdon Press, 1962) Vol. 4, pp. 787-788.

Barclay, W., *The Gospels and Acts* (London: SCM Press, 1976) 2 Vols.

Barrett, C.K., *The Gospel According to St John* (London, SPCK, 1978).

Bearsley, P., 'Mary the Perfect Disciple: A Paradigm for Mariology', *Theological Studies* 41 (1980) 461-504.

Bearsley, P., 'The Metamorphosis of Mariology', *The Clergy Review* 49 (1984) 65-71.

Betz, H.-D., *Galatians* (Hermeneia; Philadelphia: Fortress Press, 1979).

Blank, J., 'Die Verhandlung vor Pilatus: Joh 18:28 – 19:16 im Lichte der johanneischen Theologie', *Biblische Zeitschrift* 3 (1959) 60-81.

Blass, F. - Debrunner, A. - Funk, R.W., *A Greek Grammar of the New Testament and Other Early Christian Literature* (Chicago: The University of Chicago Press, 1961).

Blinzler, J., *Die Brüder und Schestern Jesu* (Stuttgarter Bibelstudien 21; Stuttgart: Katholisches Bibelwerk, 1967).

Boff, L., *The Maternal Face of God. The Feminine and Its Religious Expressions* (San Francisco: Harper & Row, 1987).

Bovon, F., *Luc le théologien. Vingt-cing ans de recherche (1950-1975)* (Neuchatal: Delachaux et Niéstle, 1978).

Brown, R.E. - Donfried, K.P. - Fitzmyer, J.A. - Reumann, J. (eds.), *Mary in the New Testament* (London: Geoffrey Chapman, 1978).

Brown, R.E., 'Luke's Description of the Virginal Conception', *Theological Studies* 35 (1974) 360-362.

Brown, R.E. *The Birth of the Messiah. A Commentary on the Infancy Narratives in Matthew and Luke* (New York: Doubleday, 1977).

Brown, R.E., *The Community of the Beloved Disciple. The Lives, Loves and Hates of an Individual Church in New Testament Times* (London: Geoffrey Chapman, 1979).

Brown, R.E., 'The Contribution of Critical Exegesis to an Understanding of Mary and Marian Doctrine', in *Biblical Exegesis and Church Doctrine* (New York: Paulist Press, 1985) pp. 86-100.

Brown, R.E., *The Gospel According to John* (The Anchor Bible 29-29a; New York: Doubleday, 1966-70) 2 Vols.

Brown, R.E., 'The Passion According to John: Chapters 18-19', *Worship 49* (1975) 126-134.

Bruce, F.F., *The Epistle to the Galatians. A Commentary on the Greek Text* (The New International Greek Testament Commentary; Exeter: Paternoster Press, 1982).

Bruce, F.F., *The Gospel of John* (Basingstoke: Pickering Paperbacks, 1983).

Buby, B., *Mary, the Faithful Disciple* (New York: Paulist Press, 1985).

Bultmann, R., *The Gospel of John. A Commentary* (Oxford: Basil Blackwell, 1971).

Burghardt, W., 'Mary in Eastern Patristic Thought', *Mariology 2* (1957) 88-153.

Burghardt, W., 'Mary in Western Patristic Thought', *Mariology 1* (1955) 109-155.

Byrne, B.J., *'Sons of God — Seed of Abraham.' A Study of the Sonship of God of all Christians in Paul against the Jewish Background* (Analecta Biblica 83; Rome: Biblical Institute Press, 1979).

Byrne, B.J., 'The Faith of the Beloved Disciple and the Community in John 20', *Journal for the Study of the New Testament* 23 (1985) 83-97.

Carroll, E., 'Survey of Recent Mariology', *Marian Studies.* Appears annually.

Cazelles, H., *Le Messie de la Bible* (Série Jésus et Jésus Christ; Paris: Desclée, 1978).

Collins, A.Y. (ed.), *Feminist Perspectives on Biblical Scholarship* (Society of Biblical Literature Centennial Publications 10; Chico: Scholars Press, 1985).

Cranfield, C.E.B., *The Epistle to the Romans* (International Critical Commentary; Edinburgh: T. & T. Clark, 1975-79) 2 Vols.

Culpepper, R., *Anatomy of the Fourth Gospel. A Study in Literary Design* (Foundation and Facets; Philadelphia: Fortress Press, 1983).

de Goedt, M., 'Un schème de révelation dans le Quatrième Evangile', *New Testament Studies* 8 (1961-62) 142-150.

de la Potterie, I., 'Il parto verginale del Verbo incarnato: "Non ex sanguinibus . . . sed ex Deo natus est" (Gv 1,13)', *Marianum* 45 (1983) 127-174.

de la Potterie, I., 'Jésus roi et juge d'après Jn 19:13 *"Ekathisen epi bematos"*,' *Biblica* 41 (1960) 317-347.

de la Potterie, I., 'La Mère de Jésus et la conception virginale du Fils de Dieu', *Marianum* 40 (1978) 41-90.

de la Potterie, I., 'La passion selon S. Jean' *Assemblées du Seigneur* 21 (1969) 21-34.

Dodd, C.H., *The Interpretation of the Fourth Gospel* (Cambridge: University Press, 1953).

Drury, C., 'Who's In, Who's Out', in M.D. Hooker - C. Hickling (eds.), *What about the New Testament? Essays in Honour of Christopher Evans* (London: SCM Press, 1975) pp. 223-233.

Duke, P.D., *Irony in the Fourth Gospel* (Atlanta: John Knox Press, 1985).

Fenton, J.C., *The Passion According to John* (London: SPCK, 1961).

Ferraro, G., *L'ora' di Cristo nel Quarto Vangelo* (Aloisiana 10; Rome: Herder, 1974).

Feuillet, A., *Jésus et sa Mère d'après les récits lucaniens de l'enfance et d'après saint Jean* (Paris: Gabalda, 1974).

Feuillet, A., 'L'Heure de la femme (Jn 16:21) et l'heure de la Mère de Jésus', *Biblica* 47 (1966) 168-184, 361-370, 557-573.

Fiorenza, E.S., *Bread Not Stone. The Challenge of Feminist Biblical Interpretation* (Boston: Beacon Press, 1984).

Fiorenza, E.S., *In Memory of Her. A Feminist Reconstruction of Christian Origins* (London: SCM Press, 1983).

Fitzmyer, J.A., 'The Virginal Conception of Jesus in the New Testament', *Theological Studies* 34 (1973) 541-575.

Flannery, A. (ed.), *Vatican Council II. The Conciliar and Post Conciliar Documents* (Dublin: Dominican Publications, 1980).

Fuller, R.H., 'The Conception/Birth of Jesus as a Christological Moment', *Journal for the Study of the New Testament* 1 (1978) 37-52.

Graystone, G., *Virgin of all Virgins: The Interpretation of Luke 1:34* (Rome: Pio X, 1968).

Haenchen, E., 'History and Interpretation in the Johannine Passion Narrative', *Interpretation* 24 (1970) 198-219.

Haenchen, E., 'Jesus vor Pilatus (Joh 18:28 – 19:16). Zur Methode der Auslegung', in *Gott und Mensch. Gesammelte Aufsätze* (Tübingen: J.C.B. Mohr [Paul Siebeck], 1965) pp. 144-156.

Haenchen, E., *John* (Hermeneia; Philadelphia: Fortress Press, 1984) 2 Vols.

Hahn, F., 'Der Prozess Jesu nach dem Johannesevangelium. Eine Redaktionsgeschichtliche Untersuchung', *Evangelisch-katholisches Kommentar zum Neuen Testament Vorbereitung* 2 (Köln: Benzinger, 1970) pp. 23-76.

Halkes, C., 'Mary and Women', *Concilium* 168 (1983) 66-73.

Harvey, A.E., *Jesus on Trial, A Study of the Fourth Gospel* (London: SPCK, 1976).

Haughton, R., *The Re-Creation of Eve* (Springfield: Templegate Publishers, 1985).

Heine, S., *Women and Early Christianity. Are the Feminist Scholars Right?* (London: SCM Press, 1987).

Hickling, C., 'On Putting Paul in his Place', in M.D. Hooker - C. Hickling (eds.), *What about the New Testament? Essays in Honour of Christopher Evans* (London: SCM Press, 1975) pp. 76-88.

Hofrichter, P., *Nicht aus Blut sondern monogen aus Gott geboren. Textkritische, dogmengeschichtliche, und exegetische Untersuchung zu John 1,13-14* (Forschung zur Bibel 31; Stuttgart: Katholisches Bibelwerk, 1978).

Horton, A., *The Child Jesus* (London: Geoffrey Chapman, 1975).

Hoskyns, E.C. - Davey, F.N. (ed.), *The Fourth Gospel* (London: Faber & Faber, 1947).

Jacques, X., *List of New Testament Words Sharing Common Elements* (Rome: Biblical Institute Press, 1969).

Jeremias, J., *Jerusalem in the Time of Jesus* (London: SCM Press, 1969).

Johnson, L.T., *The Literary Function of Possessions in Luke-Acts* (SBL Dissertation Series 39; Missoula: Scholars Press, 1977).

Johnson, M.D., *The Purpose of the Biblical Genealogies with Special Reference to the Setting of the Genealogies of Jesus* (SNTS Monograph Series 8; Cambridge: University Press, 1969).

Kingsbury, J.D., *The Christology of Mark's Gospel* (Philadelphia: Fortress Press, 1983).

Koehler, Th., Article 'Storia della Mariologia', in S. De Fiores - S. Meo (eds.), *Nuovo Dizionario di Mariologia* (Rome: Edizioni Paoline, 1985) pp. 1385-1405.

Kümmel, W.G., *Introduction to the New Testament* (London: SCM Press, 1975).

Küng, H. - Moltmann, J. (eds.), 'Mary in the Churches', *Concilium* 168 (Edinburgh, T. & T. Clark, 1983).

Laurentin, R., 'Bulletin marial', *Revue des Sciences Philosophiques et Théologiques* (1962-). Twice yearly.

Lauterbach, J.Z., 'Jesus in the Talmud' in T. Weiss-Rossmarin (ed.), *Jewish Expressions on Jesus. An Anthology* (New York: Ktav, 1967) pp. 1-98.

Lightfoot, J.B., *Saint Paul's Epistle to the Galatians* (London: Macmillan, 1884).

Lindars, B., *The Gospel of John* (New Century Bible; London: Oliphants, 1972).

Loades, A., *Searching for Lost Coins. Explorations in Christianity and Feminism* (London: SPCK, 1987).

Lozano, J.M. *Life as Parable. Reinterpreting the Religious Life* (New York: Paulist Press, 1986).

Macken, J.G., *The Virgin Birth of Christ* (London: James Clarke, 1958).

Mahoney, R., 'Die Mutter Jesu in Neuen Testament', in G. Dautzenberger - H. Merklein - K. Müller (eds.), *Die Frau im Urchristentum* (Quaestiones Disputatae 95; Herder: Freiburg, 1983) pp. 92-116.

Malatesta, E., 'Blood and Water from the Pierced Side of Christ', in P.-R. Tragan (ed.), *Segni e Sacramenti nel Vangelo di Giovanni* (Studia Anselmiana 66, Sacramentum 3; Rome: Editrice Anselmiana, 1977) pp. 164-181.

Matera, F.J., *The Kingship of Jesus. Composition and Theology in Mark 15* (SBL Dissertation Series 66; Chico: Scholars Press, 1982).

McHugh, J. *The Mother of Jesus in the New Testament* (London: Darton, Longman & Todd, 1975).

McKenzie, J.L., 'The Mother of Jesus in the New Testament', *Concilium* 168 (1983) 3-11.

Meeks, W.A., *The Prophet-King. Moses Traditions and the Johannine Christology* (Supplements to Novum Testamentum 14; Leiden: E.J. Brill, 1967).

Metzger, B.M., *A Textual Commentary on the Greek New Testament* (London/New York: United Bible Societies, 1971).

Miguens, M., *The Virgin Birth. An Evaluation of the Scriptural Evidence* (Westminster: Christian Classics, 1975).

Mollat, D., 'Jésus devant Pilate (Jean 18:28 – 19:16)', *Bible et Vie Chrétienne* 39 (1961) 23-31.

Moloney, F.J., 'From Cana to Cana (Jn 2:1 – 4:54) and the Fourth Evangelist's Concept of Correct (and Incorrect) Faith', *Salesianum* 40 (1978) 817-843. Also available in E.A. Livingstone (ed.), *Studia Biblica II. Papers on the Gospels. Sixth International Congress on Biblical Studies. Oxford 3-7 April 1978* (Sheffield: JSOT Press, 1980) pp. 185-213.

Moloney, F.J., 'Jesus Christ: The Question to Cultures', *Pacifica* 1 (1988) 15-43.

Moloney, F.J., 'John 17: The Prayer of Jesus' Hour', *The Clergy Review* 67 (1982) 79-83.

Moloney, F.J., 'John 20: A Journey Completed', *Australasian Catholic Record* 59 (1982) 417-432.

Moloney, F.J., 'Revisiting John', *Scripture Bulletin* 11 (Summer 1980) 9-15.

Moloney, F.J., 'The Infancy Narratives. Another View of Raymond Brown's *The Birth of the Messiah*', *The Clergy Review* 65 (1979) 161-166.

Moloney, F.J. *The Johannine Son of Man* (Biblioteca de Scienze Religiose 14; Rome: LAS, 1978).

Moloney, F.J., *The Living Voice of the Gospel. The Gospels Today* (Melbourne: Collins Dove, 1987).

Moloney, F.J., *The Word Became Flesh* (Theology Today Series 14; Dublin/Cork: Mercier Press, 1977).

Moloney, F.J., 'When is John Talking about Sacraments?', *Australian Biblical Review* 30 (1982) 10-33.

Moloney, F.J., *Woman: First Among the Faithful. A New Testament Study* (Melbourne: Collins Dove, 1984).

Morgan-Wynne, J.E., 'The Cross and the Revelation of Jesus as *ego eimi* in the Fourth Gospel', in E.A. Livingstone (ed.), *Studia Biblica II. Papers on the Gospels. Sixth International Congress on Biblical Studies. Oxford 3-7 April 1978* (Sheffield: JSOT Press, 1980) pp. 219-226.

Müller, A., 'Marias Stellung und Mitwirkung im Christusereignis', in J. Feiner - M. Löhrer (eds.), *Mysterium Salutis. Grundriss Heilsgeschichtlicher Dogmatik* (Einsiedeln: Benziger Verlag, 1969) Vol. 3/2, pp. 407-421.

Navone, J. - Cooper, T., *Tellers of the Word* (New York: Le Jacq Publishing, 1981).

Nicholson, G.C., *Death as Departure. The Johannine Descent-Ascent Scheme* (SBL Dissertation Series 63; Chico: Scholars Press, 1983).

Oberlinner, L., *Historischer Überlieferungen und christologische Aussage. Zur Frage der 'Brüder Jesu' in der Synopse* (Forschung zur Bibel 19; Stuttgart: Katholisches Bibelwerk; 1975).

Pellegrino, M. (ed.), S. Agostino D'Ippona: *La Vergine Maria* (Milan: Edizioni Paoline, 1987).

Pennington, M.B., *Mary Today. The Challenging Woman* (New York: Doubleday, 1987).

Pesch, R. *Das Markusevangelium* (Herders theologischer Kommentar zum Neuen Testament II/1-2; Freiburg: Herder, 1977-78) 2 Vols.

Philips, G., 'Dogmatic Constitution on the Church. History of the Constitution', in H. Vorgrimler (ed.), *Commentary on the Documents of Vatican II* (London: Burns & Oates, 1967) Vol. I, pp. 105-137.

Pintard, J., 'Le principe "prius mente quam corpore . . ." dans la patristique et la théologie latine', *Bulletin de la Societé Francaise d'Etudes Mariales* 27 (1970) 25-58.

Pope John Paul II, *Redemptoris Mater. On the Blessed Virgin Mary in the Life of the Pilgrim Church* (Vatican City: 25th March 1987).

Pope Paul VI, *Marialis Cultus. For the Right Ordering and Development of Devotion to the Blessed Virgin Mary* (Vatican City: 25th March 1974).

Ratzinger, J., *Daughter Zion. Meditations on the Church's Marian Belief* (San Francisco: Ignatius Press, 1983).

Rhoads, D. - Michie, D., *Mark as Story. An Introduction to the Narrative of a Gospel* (Philadelphia: Fortress Press, 1982).

Robinson, J.A.T., *Redating the New Testament* (London: SCM Press, 1976).

Robson, J., 'Mary: My Sister', in M. Furlong (ed.), *Feminine in the Church* (London: SPCK, 1984) pp. 119-138.

Ruether, R.R., *Mary – The Feminine Face of the Church* (Philadelphia: Westminster Press, 1977).

Ruether, R.R., *Sexism and God-Talk. Towards a Feminist Theology* (London: SCM Press, 1983).

Schlier, H., *Lettera ai Galati* (Biblioteca di Studi Biblici 3; Brescia: Paideia, 1965).

Schmaus, M., Article 'Mariology' in A. Darlap (ed.), *Sacramentum Mundi. An Encyclopedia of Theology* (London: Burns & Oates, 1968) Vol. 3, pp. 376-383.

Schnackenburg, R., *The Gospel According to St John* (London/New York: Burns & Oates/Crossroad, 1968-82) 3 Vols.

Schweizer, E., Article 'huios', *Theological Dictionary of the New Testament* VIII (1972) 363-399.

Senior, D., *The Passion of Jesus in the Gospel of Mark* (The Passion Series 2; Wilmington: Michael Glazier, 1984).

Serra, A., Article 'Bibbia' in S. De Fiores - S. Meo (eds.), *Nuovo Dizionario di Mariologia* (Roma: Edizioni Paoline, 1985) pp. 231-311. A most comprehensive bibliography of biblical Mariology can be found in this article on pp. 307-311.

Serra, A., Article 'Vergine', in S. De Fiores - S. Meo (eds.), *Nuovo Dizionario di Mariologia* (Rome: Edizioni Paoline, 1985) pp. 1424-1454. Extensive further bibliography on the virginity of Mary can be found in this article on pp. 1469-1476.

Serra, A., *Contributi dell'antica letteratura giudaica per l'esegesi di Giovanni 2:1-12 e 19:25-27* (Scripta Pontificiae Facultatis Theologicae 'Marianum' 31; Rome: Herder, 1977).

Simoens, Y., *La gloire d'aimer. Structures stylistiques et interprétatives dans la Discours de la Cène (Jn 13-17)* (Analecta Biblica 90; Rome: Biblical Institute Press, 1981).

Söll, G., *Storia dei Dogmi Mariani* (Accademia Mariana Salesiana XV; Rome: LAS, 1981).

Staniforth, M., *Early Christian Writings. The Apostolic Fathers* (Penguin Classics; Harmondsworth: Penguin Books, 1968).

Stanley, D.M., 'The Passion According to John', *Worship* 33 (1958-59) 213-230.

Stauffer, E., *Jesus and His Story* (London: SCM Press, 1960).

Stegemann, H., ' "Die des Uria": zur Bedeutung der Frauennamen in der Genealogie von Matthäus 1:1-17', in *Tradition und Glaube* (Festgabe K.G. Kuhn; Göttingen: Vandenhoeck und Ruprecht, 1972) pp. 246-276.

Tambasco, A.J., *What are they saying about Mary?* (New York: Paulist Press, 1984).

Tolbert, M.A. (ed.), *The Bible and Feminist Hermeneutics* (Semeia 28; Chico: Scholars Press, 1983).

Turner, H.E.W., 'Expository Problems: The Virgin Birth', *The Expository Times* 68 (1956-57) 12.

van den Bussche, H., *Jean. Commentaire de L'Evangile Spirituel* (Paris: Desclée de Brouwer, 1967).

van Unnik, W.C., '*Dominus Vobiscum:* The Background of a Liturgical Formula', in *New Testament Essays. Studies in Memory of Thomas Walter Manson 1893-1958* (Manchester: University Press, 1959) 270-305.

Vanhoye, A., 'La mère du fils de Dieu selon Ga 4:4', *Marianum* 40 (1978) 237-247.

Vellanickal, M., *The Divine Sonship of Christians in the Johannine Writings* (Analecta Biblica 72; Rome: Biblical Institute Press, 1977).

von Balthasar, H.-U., *Mary for Today* (Slough: St Paul Publications, 1987).

Williamson, G.A. (ed.), Eusebius, *The History of the Church from Christ to Constantine* (Minneapolis: Augsburg, 1975).

Wilson, R.R., 'Between "Azel" and "Azel". Interpreting the Biblical Genealogies', *Biblical Archeologist* 42 (1979) 11-22.

Young, F., *From Nicea to Chalcedon. A Guide to the Literature and its Background* (London: SCM Press, 1983).

Zevini, G., *Vangelo secondo Giovanni* (Commenti Spirituali del Nuovo Testamento; Rome: Città Nuova, 1984-1987) 2 Vols.

Index of Authors

Index of Biblical Passages

Made in the USA
Middletown, DE
03 February 2018